CHO[O]

LOVE

NOT

POWER

How to Right the World's Wrongs from a Place of Weakness

TONY

CAMPOLO

Regal

From Gospel Light
Ventura, California, U.S.A.

Published by Regal
From Gospel Light
Ventura, California, U.S.A.
www.regalbooks.com
Printed in the U.S.A.

First published as *The Power Delusion* by Victor Books in 1983.

Library of Congress Cataloging-in-Publication Data
Campolo, Anthony.
Choose love, not power : how to right the world's wrongs from a place of weakness /
Tony Campolo.
   p. cm.
Rev. ed. of: The power delusion. 1983.
Includes bibliographical references and index.
ISBN 978-0-8307-5124-2 (trade paper : alk. paper)
1. Power (Christian theology) 2. Authority—Religious aspects—Christianity.
   I. Campolo, Anthony. Power delusion. II. Title.
BT738.25.C35 2009
261.7—dc22
2009037878

2 3 4 5 6 7 8 9 10 / 15 14 13 12 11 10

Rights for publishing this book outside the U.S.A. or in non-English languages are
administered by Gospel Light Worldwide, an international not-for-profit ministry.
For additional information, please visit www.glww.org, email info@glww.org, or write to
Gospel Light Worldwide, 1957 Eastman Avenue, Ventura, CA 93003, U.S.A.

To Brook Gay:
A gentle, kind and joyful friend

CONTENTS

PREFACE TO THE NEW EDITION

My book entitled *The Power Delusion* was first published in 1983—and a lot has happened since then. Many of the most important insights of the feminist movement were not yet available for Christian reflection. For instance, I did not really understand the importance of inclusive language back then, and failed to see that much of what I and others in the Christian community had said and written in those days gave women a sense of being left out. I have tried to do better in this new edition and, while I still talk about God as Father, I have become aware that in God's character there is, for lack of a better term, a feminine side to God. Christian feminists have gained scholarly validation for their claim that in the Hebrew Bible (that is, the Old Testament), the word for God's Spirit is feminine and that in the New Testament, the Greek noun referring to the Holy Spirit is gender-neutral. In short, I am one of those who have come to believe that God transcends culturally defined concepts of masculinity and femininity and encompasses the best socially defined traits of both sexes. Even after making such corrections, we must all be ready to acknowledge that God is infinitely more than we could ever hope or think.

Another reason for a thorough rewrite of this book is that since 1983, power struggles between racial groups have come to be more clearly understood. African-American Christians have taught Euro-American Christians like myself a great deal about how the power we have exercised against them, ever since the days of slavery, has both oppressed them and also diminished the humanity of we white people who have done the oppressing. No discussion of how "power games" are played out in our society would be complete without some reference to how these games have affected race relations in America.

A closer look at how power games have impacted family life is also needed. Psychologists have written extensively over these past decades about how families have been affected by attempts at domination and the craving for power, and we know more now about the creation and perpetuation of destructive states of codependency. Biblical scholars have helped us to explore in greater depth what the Scriptures have to say about love and power than was available back in the early 1980s, and these insights often concur with what social scientists tell us about what makes for healthy and unhealthy familial relationships.

But we have to be careful when synthesizing biblical truths with practices sometimes prescribed by social scientists. As a case in point, some forms of modern psychology may have actually encouraged the destructive exercise of power to the detriment of relationships, both within and outside the family. Philip Rieff, in his seminal book *The Triumph of the Therapeutic*, has claimed that the psychological theories of Sigmund Freud have provided the ideological basis for a form of "self-actualization" in which individuals are given permission to assert themselves and seek hedonistic personal gratification of their libido desires, even at the expense of others.[1]

Before the work of Freud, Rieff argues, the clergy did most of the counseling. Under the auspices of religion, the clergy endeavored to carry on a "ministry of reconciliation." Their aim was to help marriages work. They attempted to help parents and children come into harmonious relationships. And ultimately, they sought to nurture persons into a surrendered relationship with God.

After Freud, these former goals for counseling were sometimes replaced by encouraging individuals to become assertive in ways that would break the "chains of approval from others" and to live out their inner desires, regardless of what emotional costs others might have to pay as that individual strove to actualize the potentialities of the self.

Fredrick Nietzsche would call such behavior "the will to power," and it is essential for us to explore how contrary this is to sacrificial love that is at the core of Christianity.

Finally, biblical scholars and theologians, since 1983, have provided more in-depth analyses of how power and love work themselves out in the lives of Christians, especially as they seek ways to become more like Christ. There is little question that our failure to understand how power plays condition the ways Christians interact with each other within the Church, as well as the ways they impact our relationships with those outside the Church, has led to contemporary distortions of Christianity from what it was intended to be. It is my hope that what follows in this book will not only lead to a better grasp of how godly people should handle power in their various spheres of life, but also will provide some helpful insights as to what the Scriptures are trying to teach us about how to live out our faith in everyday life.

POWER PLAYS
IN THE PEACEABLE
KINGDOM

One day, after finishing my lectures at a downtown university, I was driving home on the Schuylkill Expressway in Philadelphia. I had just crossed City Line Avenue when I heard a "kerplunk" and knew I had a flat tire. I tried to pull my car over to the side of the road, but if you know anything about the Schuylkill Expressway, you know that the shoulder of that expressway is so inadequate that you really can't get an automobile completely off the highway. I did the best I could.

I jacked up the car and began to change the tire—sweaty work on a fairly hot day. While I was doing all of this, I had the car radio turned on and blaring away. Over the airwaves came news from the "Go Patrol" helicopter that hovers over the city at rush hour, broadcasting to motorists the locations of traffic tie-ups. I heard the man from the Go Patrol announce, "Well, folks! They're not going to get home tonight! They're tied up on the Schuylkill Expressway all the way back to Montgomery Avenue. They're standing still in both directions on City Line Avenue. It's gridlock out there, people! Everything is standing still! Nothing is moving! The city of Philadelphia is coming to a standstill!"

As I heard this dire announcement, I thought to myself, *What evil has befallen my fair city? What catastrophe has come upon the City of Brotherly Love?*

Then the man on the radio said, "There's a brown car just west of City Line Avenue . . ."

That's my car! I realized with surprise. My *car has the city of Philadelphia tied up! My car that has created the gridlock!* I'm *the one who's created this catastrophe!* I felt like crying out in anguish, "Children are crying for their parents! Lovers are not meeting! Business deals are falling through . . . and I AM MAKING IT HAPPEN!"

Power! Who can help but enjoy the thrill of it?

The problem is that power can corrupt. The Greek tragedian Euripides is credited with the observation that "whom the gods would destroy, they first make drunk with power." And most of us remember Lord Acton's contention that absolute power corrupts absolutely.

There are few things that prove more intoxicating than power, and Christians are not immune to being seduced into playing power games. There is an excitement that comes from controlling, dominating and affecting what goes on in other people's lives.

Christians do not always take warnings about power seriously.

There are husbands who think it is their right to exercise power over their wives, and there are wives who, in subtle and not-so-subtle ways, play power games with their husbands.

There are children who try to exercise power as they challenge the controlling efforts of their parents, and there are parents who regularly tyrannize their children.

There are pastors who try to dominate their parishioners, and church members who try to manipulate their pastors.

There are employers who enjoy bossing their employees, and employees who form unions just so they can strike back and dictate policies to their employers.

There are white people who fear losing their power over African-Americans, and African-Americans who turn cries of "Freedom now!" into shouts of "Black power!"

There are politicians who compromise anything to stay in power, and there are candidates who, in challenging those politicians, use any deception to wrest power from the incumbents.

There are nations that, in order to become world powers, willingly threaten the survival of the human race by building war machines, and there are world leaders who would push the buttons for all-out nuclear war if they thought their power was being threatened.

The German philosopher Fredrick Nietzsche understood that human beings are hungry for power. Nietzsche declared that "the will to power" is the basic human drive and the essence of our humanity. On this issue, Nietzsche was a forerunner of Sigmund Freud who, in his early writings, tried to explain all human behavior as an attempt to satisfy sexual appetites—the "will to pleasure." I am convinced that Nietzsche was much closer to the truth than Freud in his understanding of human nature; I believe he would have claimed that much of what goes on in sexual relationships has little to do with gratifying libido urges. Instead, it has to do with power.

Much of what goes on sexually between partners can be understood as people exercising domination. Many psychologists and marital counselors report that, in far too many of the marriages they deal with in their professional practices, there are too many power games and too little love. Sometimes even rape occurs within marriage. The extreme act of sexual power is rape, which, as most feminists point out, is an act of power in which one person gets gratification by humiliating, controlling and dominating another.

Nietzsche, with his atheistic understanding of human nature, claimed that people have a craving to control their own destinies and to be free to realize their individualistic potential without restraints from anyone. To be free from all limitations, he contended, is an ultimate aspiration. He championed the concept of the "superman," who would transcend the proscriptions of society and God and shrug off responsibility towards others if such responsibilities interfered with his or her personal goals.

I personally think that Nietzsche rejected any notion of God because he could not tolerate the thought of anyone more powerful than himself. But while I am diametrically opposed to Nietzsche's atheistic beliefs, I have to agree that persons apart from the transforming influence of Christ are very much as Nietzsche described them. Many social scientists, myself included, believe that his understanding of human nature is more profound and far-reaching than any other that has since emerged. Strangely, to some of us, what this enemy of Christianity observed about unredeemed human nature is very much in harmony with what the Bible teaches. What the Christian theologians call our "fallen nature" is very much oriented to playing power games.

The case can be made that the most important consequence of surrendering to the transforming influence of Christ in our lives is that we begin to undergo a process whereby we can be delivered from what Nietzsche described as the will to power and made into persons who, like Christ, are willing to give up power in order to express love. Giving up power, as I will later point out, is a requisite for loving. Fallen humanity, however, apart from the redemptive work of Christ, is very much as Nietzsche described it: completely obsessed with power. In other words, humans are a bunch of control freaks.

Nietzsche clearly saw that hunger for power is anti-Christian. He recommended the "slaves" should kill the "slave master": God. He declared that Christianity should be abolished because it asks people to surrender to God, to render themselves as weak vessels to be used of the Lord and to refuse to exercise power over others. He understood more clearly than most Christians that there is something about the craving for power that cannot be reconciled with a Christian lifestyle. He recognized that Christ's call to servanthood and humility precludes power games and that Christ asks us to live contrary to our fallen nature through the indwelling presence of the Holy Spirit.

Christianity is for people who want to make love the foundation of their lives. Because of this, Fredrick Nietzsche called Christians creatures with a herd mentality who are unwilling to rise above the masses to actualize their potential for greatness. As he read the story of Cain and Abel (see Gen. 4), Nietzsche declared Cain to be the superior of the two. He gladly acknowledged that he himself bore the mark of Cain and that, like Cain, would not tolerate anyone who might hinder his self-actualization through his will to power. It is no wonder that he referred to himself as the anti-Christ.

POWER VS. AUTHORITY

While this book may sound so far like it's going to be heavy philosophy, once we get past essential definitions and start applying the principles of the gospel as they relate to love and power, we'll get down to where the rubber meets the road. I'll do my best to show how the misuse of power can lead us to make serious mistakes in everyday life and how, by living out Christ's love in our relationships with others, we can be cured of the destructive power games we are prone to playing with each other.

Before I go any further, it is important that I specify how I am using the word "power." I differentiate *power* from something even more important, which is *authority*. Max Weber, one of the most prominent historical figures in the field of sociology and the author of the book *The Theory of Social and Economic Organization*, provided what have become, for social scientists, classical differentiations between the two concepts.[1] Weber asserted that *power* is the prerogative to control what happens—it is to have the coercive force to make others yield to one's wishes, even against their will. That coercive force does not have to actually be utilized by the person in power; people yield to those who have power over them because they know that the coercive force is always there, ready to be used.

For example, when I am speeding down an interstate highway and a state trooper in a patrol car pulls up behind me and turns on his flashing red lights to indicate that I should pull my car over to the shoulder of the road, I obey. I really don't want to, but I do it because I know the state trooper has power. That power exists in the form of a gun. The trooper doesn't have to pull the gun out of his holster. There is no need for him to use his gun. All that prompts me to obey is knowing that it's there and that it can be used should I refuse to comply with his directives. I obey because I have to!

On the other hand, according to Weber, *authority* is established when someone is able to elicit compliance because others *want* to obey. Others recognize a person with authority as having a legitimate right to expect compliance. My mother, for instance, had great authority over me, even though she did not have much power. She was a tiny Italian woman and I could have kicked her down a flight of steps. But such an obscene possibility would never have crossed my mind; when my mother spoke, I obeyed. I did what she told me to do because I owed her obedience.

Where did my mother get her authority? She earned it through sacrificial love. Over the years, she had done thousands and thousands of loving things to help me and nurture me along life's way. Her loving sacrifices had established her authority and the right to be obeyed.

Loving sacrifices always earn authority. With that in mind, we can easily understand why Jesus confronts Christians as if He has the ultimate authority in time and eternity. In Jesus, we find a revelation of one who gave up power, left the right hand of His Father and broke into history in order to lovingly sacrifice Himself for our salvation. In Philippians 2, we read that He had all the power of God at His disposal, yet He set it aside and took upon Himself "the very nature of a servant" (v. 7). Actually, the word "servant" is a translation of the Greek word *doulos*, which means "slave." And we all know how much power a slave has. The Scripture tells us that Jesus "humbled Himself and became obedient to death—even death on a cross" (v. 8). In the Greek New Testament, we find that the word "humbled" is *kenosis*, which means "set aside" or "emptied." Jesus emptied Himself of power because He wanted to save the world through sacrificial love. He wanted people like you and me to become the persons He wants us to be—not because we are coerced to do so, but because we want to.

If any of us become obedient Christians, it is not because Jesus twists our arms and forces us to do His will. Quite to the contrary: Jesus calls us to obey Him in response to His loving sacrifices for us. He wants us to obey Him out of love, and this is something we feel inwardly constrained to do because of what He did for us on Calvary.

When Jesus spoke, He was not like Pilate or Herod or Caesar. They had power. When He spoke, He did so as one having authority (see Mark 1:22). But shying away from power was not always easy for Him. From the beginning of His ministry until His crucifixion, Satan worked on Jesus non-stop, tempting Him to save the world through the exercise of power. But on every occasion, Jesus resisted this temptation and remained committed to saving the world through sacrificial love.

When we read in Luke 4 the story of Jesus' temptations at the hands of Satan, we see Him turning away from the allure of power. Satan asked Him to turn stones into bread—to establish His kingdom through exercising economic power. Satan told Him that, by using His power to provide for people's basic economic necessities, He could control them. But Jesus said no.

Then, Satan tried to tempt Jesus by proposing that He use religious power to establish His kingdom. Satan suggested He should jump from the highest pinnacle of the Temple on Mt. Zion and then float gently to the ground. The idea was that Jesus could get the religious leaders of Israel to become His followers by showing them some "signs and wonders"—and the masses soon would follow. But Jesus said no to religious power.

Finally, Satan took Jesus to the top of a high mountain and laid before Him all the kingdoms of the world. In this third temptation, Jesus was offered political power. He was told that He could impose His will on the world if He just would take advantage of the political power at His disposal. Again, Jesus said no.

Jesus *would* save the world, but not through power. His would not be a kingdom built on any form of coercion. Instead, He said to time and history that in being lifted up on a cross, He would draw all humanity to Himself. Jesus made it clear that His plan was for people to respond to His ultimate sacrifice of love (see John 12:32).

Right up until the end of Jesus' life on earth, Satan tried to lure Jesus to use His power. When Peter called for Jesus to seize power and establish His kingdom that way, Jesus sensed Satan tempting Him through His friend and disciple. It was in that context that Jesus said to Peter, "Get behind me, Satan!" (Matt. 16:23). But Satan did not let up—not even when Jesus was hanging on the cross. The evil one then spoke through the crowd that mocked Jesus: "Come down from the cross, if you are the Son of God!" (Matt. 27:40). The religious leaders also mocked Him, saying, "He can't save himself! He's the King of Israel! Let him come down now from the cross, and we will believe in him" (Matt. 27:42). They called on Him to demonstrate His power, but Jesus resisted.

Christian activists often delude themselves into thinking that the kingdom of God can be actualized in history through the use of political power. They say, "If only our people are elected to office—if only we can gain control of the mechanisms of political power—then we can make our country into the kind of nation God wants it to be. Through political power, we can overcome those things that we believe offend God."

The Religious Right says, "If we had the power, we could end abortion and stop gay marriages."

The Religious Left says, "If we had the power, we could end poverty, save the environment and put an end to war."

All too frequently, Christian activists at both ends of the political spectrum see power as the primary instrument for saving the world. "If we just had the power," they say, "we could set everything right."

I want to say to them, "I wonder why Jesus didn't think of that! Why didn't Jesus understand that with political power the nation could be saved? Why didn't Jesus think of coming as a Caesar with a mighty army and imposing His will on humanity?"

We all know the answer to such questions. Jesus chose a harder way. He chose the way of the cross. He would save the world not through power, but through sacrificial love. And with that sacrificial love, He would earn the authority to call all of humanity into obedience to His will.

None of what I am trying to say discounts the role of power in restraining evil and enacting justice, as will be pointed out later in this book. What is being argued here is that when the Church takes on the role of exercising political power, it no longer follows the way of Jesus and loses its authority.

DEMONSTRATIONS OF AUTHORITY

I have seen authority established through sacrificial love time and time again in our modern world. There was the time when Mother Teresa spoke at a Harvard University graduation. She lectured the Harvard students on sexual morality—you have to admit that that is a courageous thing to do in the "Halls of Ivy." The students sat in rapt attention. They did not hiss or try to shout her down. That is because, when she spoke, she spoke as one having authority. And we all know where she got that authority. She got it on the streets of Calcutta, ministering to the sick and dying. She gained her authority as she sacrificially gave herself to meet the needs of the poorest of the poor, to comfort the sick and to give dignity to the dying.

Working with the Evangelical Association for the Promotion of Education (EAPE), the organization to which I am primarily committed in Christian service, I was able to recruit a young doctor by the name of Elias Santana. He provided me with another example of how authority could be established through sacrificial love. This bright and dynamic Christian graduated from medical school and, living in the Chicago area, could easily have earned a small fortune by setting up a medical practice that took care of middle-class Americans. Instead, under the conviction of the Holy Spirit, Elias decided to return to his home country, the Dominican Republic, and establish the Dominican branch of the Christian Medical Society.

Elias regularly traveled from his home country to Puerto Rico, where he performed surgery for those who had the money to pay high fees for his services. He then would return home and, with the money he had earned in Puerto Rico, buy medical supplies. He would then give out these supplies for free to the poor in the slums of Santo Domingo.

One day I went with this servant of God to one of the worst slums in the city. I stood by throughout the day, watching him freely serve those who had no means to pay. He gave away expensive medicines to those who could not afford to buy them. After a day of sacrificially living out Christ's love, Elias climbed to the top of his truck and yelled for the people in the *barrio* to gather around. I watched and listened as he preached the gospel story and called people to surrender their lives to Christ.

Standing at the edge of the crowd, I noticed a young man who went by the name of Socrates. He was the head of the Che Guevara Society, the leftist student organization on the campus of the Universidad Autónoma de Santo Domingo. I knew Socrates to be a good-hearted person, but one who had embraced an erroneous ideology. He cared about poor people and wanted his country to bring justice and hope to the poor, but his method was to join with those who wanted a revolution to establish a new social order by means of power.

I went over to Socrates and jokingly nudged him and said as I pointed to Elias standing on the truck, "Socrates! Elias is winning converts! If he keeps this up, he will sway this crowd to being Christian, and there will be nobody left for you to convert to your Marxist ideology."

I will never forget Socrates's answer. With his teeth clenched (I could not tell whether from anger or admiration), he said, "What can I say? Elias Santana has earned the right to be heard."

Elias Santana, in a Christ-like fashion, spoke with authority.

Jesus will establish His kingdom here on earth, and He will do so through the authority flowing from His sacrificial love. Unlike the dictators that often emerge from proletarian revolutions, He will not suppress His opposition nor coerce people to comply with His wishes. Unlike those so-called "liberators" like Lenin and Castro, who tried to establish a better world through power, our Jesus shows us the way of the cross. He says that if we would be His disciples, each of us must likewise take up a cross and follow Him (see Matt. 16:24). He calls us to imitate Him by living out sacrificial love so that we might have the authority that can change the world.

Right now, the Church in America does not speak with much authority. Most people know that it has amassed huge financial resources that have been used for the aggrandizement of its own institutions. Billions have been spent to construct buildings for a God who "does not live in temples built by hands," according to Acts 17:24. If the Church had instead used its vast resources sacrificially on behalf of the poor and needy, I am convinced that the world would be listening to us with more attention than we can imagine.

It's been said that the Church should be the only club in the world that exists for the benefit of its non-members. People should see us as having "the mind of Christ" (1 Cor. 2:16) as we empty ourselves of power and live sacrificially to meet the needs of others. We should always keep in mind that the Christ who put aside His power and humbled Himself unto death—the ultimate act of sacrificial love—ultimately triumphs in history. That passage in Philippians 2, partially quoted earlier, ends with these words:

> Therefore God exalted him to the highest place and gave him the name that is above every name, that at the name of Jesus every knee should bow, in heaven and on earth and under the earth, and every tongue confess that Jesus Christ is Lord, to the glory of God the Father (Phil. 2:9-11).

But His triumph is a triumph of love. The world is saved through love, and power is used only to restrain what love cannot redeem.

THE PROPER USE OF POWER

The destructive, egoistic use of power can have devastating consequences. A contrast to Jesus, who willingly set aside His divine power when He came into the world to express His love, is Satan. The evil one lusted for power and, according to Christian tradition, it brought about his downfall. The fact that God the Father had power greater than his proved intolerable. This led him to seek ways to usurp the position of the heavenly King.

The great English poet, John Milton, explored the motivations that lay behind Satan's rebellion against God in his epic poem *Paradise Lost*. In that poem, Milton has Satan say, "To reign is worth ambition though in hell. Better to reign in hell than serve in Heav'n." Satan could not accept being less than all-powerful. His will to power necessitated his being thrown out of heaven.

Here on earth, Satan tempted Adam and Eve and instilled in them a desire for power, which allowed them to be seduced into sin. Satan told that first couple that if they ate the fruit of the Tree of the Knowledge of Good and Evil, which God has forbidden, they would be like gods (see Gen. 3). The original couple found this possibility too enticing to resist. Thus, we learn from Scripture, original sin was born out of their jealousy for God's power. It was their will to power that brought the curse of sin and suffering upon the human race.

But even as we discuss the dangers inherent in possessing power, we ought to recognize that power *can* be used in a positive manner. It is especially effective in restraining evil; thus, God gives rulers and government power to do just that. In Romans 13, we are told that those who have power given to them by God to rule over society are called on to hold evil in check. Let's be clear: Governments that restrain evil cannot bring salvation to the world. They can, however, hold those demonic forces in check that would otherwise raise havoc and destruction in the lives of individuals and society. The Bible tells us that these rulers do not wield the sword in vain, but are called on to execute God's wrath on those who do evil (see Rom. 13:4). Those who have political power through government cannot bring about the spiritual transformation that is essential for kingdoms of this world to become the kingdom of our God, but they can hold back death and destruction perpetrated by people of evil intent. Even Dietrich Bonhoeffer, pacifist pastor though he was, realized when the time had come in Nazi Germany to use power to try to stop Hitler from destroying the world.[2]

Power has its place, and I thank God for those Christians who are willing to take positions in government. I praise God for those Christians who wield government power to root out the evil that has crept into our political and economic institutions, and bring about social reform. But the spiritual transformation of humanity, which is the basis of God's kingdom, requires acts of sacrificial love. We should never count on those in government to be the primary instruments for bringing about the kingdom of God on earth. This is the task of the Church. I do not mean the institutional Church; I mean the Church as the people of God at work in the world, living out sacrificial love.

There is nothing inherently evil about power. Remember that one of these days, the Jesus who lived out sacrificial love 2,000 years ago, and continues to live out His love through His people in the here and now, is coming back. There will be an event, which we affirm in the Apostles' Creed, called the Second Coming. And when Christ does return, He will return in power. Christ used power in casting out demons and when there was evil to be destroyed, but it was always through sacrificial love that He sought to bring His salvation to His world and to its people. Christ's love is so evident in that many of us forget that our Lord also carries in His back pocket incredible power, and that this power will be released on the world on the Day of Judgment. He will use His power to put down all evil and extinguish all uncleanness and corruption. Upon His return, those who have rejected His love will run to the hills and wish that they had never been born. Read Matthew 24 if you want to get a glimpse of the horrific consequences that will befall those who do not respond to sacrificial love. On that final day, all evil shall be put down and Christ shall reign in love forever and ever. That is why we shout "Hallelujah!" as that day approaches.

LOVE AND POWER IN THE FAMILY

Christopher Lasch, in his book *Haven in a Heartless World*, contends that there is an illusion that the home is a place of peace and renewal for people who have endured oppression and put-downs in the workplace. Those who go to work every day and live in that "dog-eat-dog world," in which so many play power games in order to advance themselves even at the expense of others, are supposed to be able, at the end of the day, to retreat into their own little castle where there is peace and harmony. The home is supposed to be a safe place with protective walls to keep the hostilities of the world away.[1]

Yet such is not reality. There are constant reports that some of the worst emotional battlegrounds these days are not in the workplace, but are located in the context of family life. People return to their "safe" homes, in so many cases, only to find them filled with tension, arguments and hostility, as people in the family seek to play power games with each other. Husbands and wives try to control each other. Children seek to assert themselves against the authority of their parents. Sibling rivalry has children trying to dominate each other. In so many homes, individuals try to have their own way to the detriment of loving relationships. More and more, we hear about women and men who work outside the home in order to minimize their time with other family members; they find that the tensions in the household are too painful to handle.

For such reasons, we must turn our attention to how power and sacrificial love play themselves out in American homes, and the difference that Christ can make when He gains authority over the hearts and minds of parents and children.

THE PRINCIPLE OF LEAST INTEREST

Willard Waller, an often-neglected American sociologist, did most of his writings during the first half of the twentieth century. His brilliant insights into family life were largely ignored until Christopher Lasch later rediscovered his work. What Waller had to say about marriage and familial relationships is incredibly relevant to a Christian understanding of family life.

Waller's own marriage, like his parents', was a disaster. After years of bitterness and pain, he and his wife divorced. As he studied what had gone wrong in his own marriage and in the marriages of others, he became aware that many married people, even when not opting for divorce, suffered from profound unhappiness. Those who stayed together only did so because of religious reasons or societal obligations. Waller was amazed at how many unhappy marriages he came across in his studies, and he tried to discover the causes behind all of this misery and sadness. He found his answer in the craving for power inherent in human nature.

In destructive dating and marriage, Waller observed that each of the partners was endeavoring to gain power over the other. He also observed that *one way to gain this power was to withhold love*. This discovery became the basis for his theoretical understanding of the relationship between love and power. He called this insight the "principle of least interest."[2] Waller contended that in any relationship, the person who has the most power exercises the least amount of love, and that the person who loves the most has the least power.

All of us have seen the principle of least interest expressed in real-life situations. In dating, the partner who loves least and is least-interested in continuing the relationship is in a position to exercise control and determine the conditions of the relationship. Think of a high-school girl who is desperately in love. Her boyfriend, on the other hand, has only a limited interest in her. It does not take much to figure out that in such a situation, he is able to exercise great power over her and can make her do almost anything he wants her to do. She obeys his wishes because she is afraid to lose him. She may even submit to sexual relations with him, in spite of the fact that pre-marital sex is contrary to her religious convictions. Because she is so romantically turned on to him and because he loves her so little, she ends up powerless. She desperately wants to continue the relationship at all costs, and so she is vulnerable to his every whim. This dynamic is the reason every mother gets nervous when her daughter, away at university, calls home and says, "I've found a special person and I am in love with him." The mother wonders whether or not being in love has made her daughter vulnerable to manipulation by her new boyfriend. The mother worries about the possibility of exploitation.

Without ever learning about Waller's principle of least interest, most young people instinctively understand how it works. In dating, each is cautious about loving the other too much, for fear of consequences. Each tries to get the other person to love the most, and neither dares to love without reservation until he or she has assurance of being loved equally in return. A young man might develop what, in my day, we called a "line." This is a way of talking aimed at convincing the young woman that he loves her more than he really does. He might tell her that he has never felt this way with anyone before, that he has never experienced anything like the love surging through him, that he never knew that love could be so wonderful, and on and on. His line, however, may be nothing more than a deceitful way to seduce the girl. And if she buys the line and risks giving him her love, he has her right where he wants her. The rest, as they say, is history.

The young woman, on the other hand, may not be so naïve. She may have learned the hard way not to believe everything she hears from such a suitor. She may be all too aware of the stakes in this game and of what she stands to lose. With caution, she may parry the line and pride herself on her ability to not be taken in. Her game may be to get him to be in love with her without allowing herself to become too emotionally involved with him in advance.

And so, the game is played: each person trying to love less; each withholding love in order to gain power over the other; each afraid to love because it would mean the loss of power.

When this game is described with clarity, its horrible character is exposed. We see that what God meant to be a mutually gratifying relationship can be perverted into a destructive power struggle. Instead of following God's design to love each other, people instead play power games by withholding love. Sadly, this game is often played out even after marriage. Almost every counselor can tell you about couples in which one or both partners are afraid to love because they fear the consequences of losing power. Coming into the marriage, they are already so effective at withholding love that they cannot stop doing it after the wedding. We'll never know how many marriages break up because of this.

Being afraid to express love begins early in life. I can remember telling one of my eighth-grade friends that I really liked a particular girl. It was one of the worst things I could have done. My friend threatened to tell her and I almost died out of fear of embarrassment. I told him I would do anything he wanted as long as he kept secret how much I liked that girl. My friend got a lot of mileage out of that offer.

What was I afraid of anyway? What was it that so horrified me? The answer is simple: I was afraid she would know that I liked her without first knowing if she liked me. If she didn't like me, I would have been vulnerable. She might even have laughed at me, and I would have been powerless to prevent my humiliation. I would rather she never knew that I liked her than to take that chance. She never found out how I felt about her. Who knows? We might have really hit it off, but there's a price for remaining invulnerable.

The game continues in high school. Edgar Friedenberg tells us, in his excellent book on teenage life, *Coming of Age in America*, that high school status is determined by how many persons of the opposite sex a teenager can get to fall for him or her.[3] According to this theory, popularity in school is dependent on nothing more than turning on members of the opposite sex without falling in love in return. In the subculture of the high school, young people are conditioned to prefer power to love. The amount of sexual exploitation that goes on in American high schools because of this conditioning is shocking. (Some find it is easy to make the case for keeping teenaged boys and girls in separate high schools based on this dynamic.)

Fifty years ago, when Elvis Presley sang his pleading song, "Don't Be Cruel," he gave expression to what so many young people still experience in their love lives today. In loving, they realize that they have become vulnerable to the abuse of partners who exploit their love with power that they gain from loving less.

ICONS OF POWER IN RELATIONSHIPS

One of the ugly consequences of preferring power to love is what can be called "the Don Juan syndrome." There are some men who get great satisfaction in persuading a long succession of women to fall head-over-heels in love with them while they, the men, remain emotionally detached. They take pride in their ability to bring women under their control while keeping themselves free from involvement. These men view the women who prove susceptible to their seductions as conquests but, like the legendary Don Juan, they never experience the gratifications that come from genuine love. They are afraid to love because they know that loving will make them vulnerable to the same callous treatment that they have perpetrated on others.

Such men are never really satisfied with their conquests; their power plays always leave them hungry for more conquests and more power. Sadly, they almost always establish a style of relating to women that never allows them the fulfillment of a loving relationship. Their shallow victories leave them empty because in their efforts to bring women under their control, they lose the capacity to love.

It is important to recognize that men are not the only ones guilty of viewing members of the opposite sex as objects to be conquered rather than persons to be loved. There are women who also play this game, who seek to bring men under their control without really loving them. I refer to such women as suffering from "the Carmen syndrome." Such women play with men's emotions and, like Carmen in Bizet's opera, mock the cravings of the men even as they seek to possess them. They flirt and entice, and then abandon the men who are seduced by their wiles. What they don't realize is that they are victimized by their own indifference and cruelty; they are losing the capacity to love while playing their power games.

The James Bond movies pick up the same theme. Bond, also known as Agent 007 of the British Secret Intelligence Service, is able to get women to fall in love with him while he remains cool and detached. In doing so, he gains power over them and can often persuade them to provide him with sexual pleasures and then lead them into betraying their former loyalties. Women become his tools for pursuing his goals.

Unfortunately, James Bond has become the model for far too many men in the Western world. Being cool or emotionally detached has become a trait that many men want to imitate. The problem with the James Bonds of the world is that they usually play at being cool for so long that they lose the capacity to ever be passionate. Passion requires that the individual surrender to the desires of his or her partner. This the imitators of James Bond will never do because they are deluded into thinking that it is better to have power over women than to be passionately surrendered to them in love.

Deborah Tannen, a well-known linguist, has written several books that explore male/female differentiations in respect to power.[4] Among her many examples of the power practices of men, she points out that, generally speaking, men are afraid to ask directions. On a car trip, they tend to get lost. For a man to stop at a gas station and ask an attendant for directions is for him to acknowledge that he is powerless to find his way. To yield power is something that most men find very difficult to do. Consequently, a man lost in his travels will often ask his wife to go in and ask for directions.

Women, on the other hand, are more socialized not to be bothered by power games. They find it easier to ask a sometimes gruff man inside a service station how to get to where they want to go. (Tannen jokes that the reason the children of Israel were lost in the wilderness for 40 years was because Moses, a man, was unwilling to ask for directions; it took the Wise Men so long to find their way to the Baby Jesus for the same reason.)

Knowledge is power, and men who are nurtured by society to be macho are often reluctant to admit that they lack knowledge and the power that goes with it. Upon reflection, I can easily come up with examples of this in my own life. As a case in point, I remember seeing the Swedish art film *The Seventh Seal* with my wife. The movie is overwhelmed with symbols, metaphors and allegories. After seeing it, my wife asked me what all the signs and symbols alluded to and what they meant. In my socially conditioned chauvinistic manner, I explained to her the subtle meanings of all that had flashed on the silver screen—in spite of the fact that I didn't understand what was going on any better than she did. I had fallen prey to the male mystique of power. Pretending to understand, I was trying to put myself in a superior position of power. Showing her ability to see through my feeble attempts to appear knowledgeable, my wife remarked, "I thought you didn't know!"

POWER AND LOVE IN MARRIAGE

Men in particular have been deluded into the temptation to be powerful, and some end up wanting to dominate their wives. The role of being "in charge" has been socially prescribed for husbands; even in our post-feminist era it is still a part of our folk culture. Sometimes men are led to think that a Christian husband is merely a spiritualized version of a "macho man." They have heard too many misguided sermons from preachers who proclaim that God designed women to want to be dominated. And as they have tried to bring their wives into "submission," according to what they believe to be biblical teachings, such men have limited their capacity to love.

I am dismayed by the number of Christian women who have complained in counseling sessions that their husbands never tell them that they love them. I heard of one husband who, responding to such a complaint, said, "Twenty-eight years ago when I married her, I told her that I loved her and that if I ever changed my mind, I would let her know." Such a husband recognizes that expressing love diminishes his power to dominate and believes that dominating is exactly what the Bible teaches him to do. Yet the Scriptures say that husbands are supposed to love their wives as Christ loved the Church and gave Himself for it (see Eph. 5:25). To love one's wife is to live in a vulnerable condition—after all, Christ made Himself vulnerable when He suffered and died on behalf of His loved ones! Furthermore, the man who loves does not seek to have his own way and dominate, because love just doesn't do that (see 1 Cor. 13:5).

Too many husbands have been socialized to view being overtly loving as contrary to being manly. They are so conditioned that they would rather be "real men," as chauvinistically defined, than to love. Satan deludes such men with the will to power and, as they yield to this delusion, they lose the capacity for the greatest of all human joys: the thrill of surrendering in a loving relationship.

This craving for power is so overriding for some men that it even ruins their ability to enjoy a healthy sex life. The sex act ceases to be a means for expressing love and becomes instead an exercise in demonstrating power. Every marriage counselor I have talked to reports cases wherein husbands failed to be aroused unless they can reduce their wives to servile and humiliating behavior. Their aphrodisiac is power. Love does not stimulate them; only the exercise of power does. Many women too often and for too long have had to endure degradation at the hands of their husbands and have allowed such practices to continue unchallenged. Just because a couple is legally married does not give a husband the right to turn their sexual relationship into a humiliating power game. Some Christian men have taken the verse "Wives submit to your husbands" (Eph. 5:22) to mean that their wives should willingly submit to any indignity that will stoke the husband's perverted sense of power.

There is a lot of rape going on in so-called Christian marriages. Seldom do people talk about it, but I am talking about it now and saying as clearly as I can that God condemns such behavior. Those who believe that women are ordered by God to submit to such dehumanization dishonor God's image fingerprinted on each of His daughters.

Over the years, I have occasionally delivered lectures on Christian marriage. During the question-and-answer time, it has become almost inevitable that some man will stand up and ask, "Doctor! You haven't answered the real question! Who is supposed to be *head of the house*?"

Whenever that question is asked, I always have a strong temptation to say, "A Christian would never ask a question like that!" A Christian never asks who is going to be the head or the master of the house. Instead, the Christian asks if he can be a servant. The Christian knows that Jesus taught, "If anyone wants to be first, he must be the very last, and the servant of all" (Mark 9:35).

There are husbands who love to remind their wives of the apostle Paul's teaching: "the husband is the head of the wife as Christ is the head of the church" (Eph. 5:23). Yes, the Bible clearly states that wives should submit to their husbands; but if you read the rest of that chapter, you find that husbands are supposed to love their wives just as Christ loved the Church and gave Himself for it (see Eph. 5:25). And we have already seen how Jesus loved the Church: by emptying Himself of power and becoming its servant (or, as it says in the Greek, its slave). Now I have to ask: *What woman would have any trouble submitting completely to a man who defined himself as her slave?* What is called for in Christian marriage is for husbands and wives to submit themselves "to one another" (Eph. 5:21), and that each should esteem the other person ahead of himself or herself.

The questioner at my lecture is likely then to ask who is supposed to make the everyday decisions in the household. Who should to be in control? Not to be overly simplistic, but my answer is, *Why not let Jesus be head of the house?* Why not have a marriage in which both husband and wife search Scripture and go before the Lord in prayer, seeking His will in the decision-making process? In the kingdom Christ is creating, there is a very special kind of equality between husbands and wives. Mutual submission is the model for Christian marriage: the husband and wife together seeking the will of God, with neither seeking to dominate or control.

When we begin to work out Christian discipleship in the context of marriage, a complete restructuring of the family is called for. As citizens of His kingdom, we shy away from the old patriarchy and move into an era of mutual companionship. Both men and women must rethink what it means to be married, to be in love and to relinquish power to one another.

As we move forward in this book, I will propose additional—and what may seem like dramatic—changes for the ways Christian men and women interact with each other. I hope you will judge for yourself whether or not these proposals are biblical.

WOMEN WITH POWER

Men are not the only ones who play power games. I have already alluded to the reality that women play them, too. But because our society has a value system that considers it improper for women to be aggressive or even assertive (there is a difference), they often play their power games with great subtlety. Some women are able to use their physical attractiveness to exercise power over men. They realize that they can control men through sexual allurements. Undoubtedly, many a man in the old days was manipulated down the aisle because it was the only way he could get what he wanted from the woman who turned him on sexually. Only a few decades ago, mothers actually taught their daughters to use sex in such a manner, because "if you give yourself to him without him marrying you, he never will. After all, why should he marry when he can get what he wants without marrying?" Sentiments like that suggest a low view of marriage and provide a somewhat unfair judgment of men. Teaching girls that sex is something to be used to get men to do what they want has all kinds of ugly connotations.

Some women have been known to withhold sex from their husbands in order to gain power over them, not realizing that when they do so, they may be victimized by their own schemes. Such women can become sexually frigid because they become reluctant to "let themselves go" with their husbands. They become conditioned to associate the withholding of sex with power and are afraid to be passionate with their spouses—they are afraid to lose power and become vulnerable. Sadly, some of these women only overcome their sexual inhibitions through infidelity; having sex on a one-night stand with a stranger, they experience the sexual release they are incapable of experiencing with their marriage partners. The woman knows that the stranger will not have power over her once the sexual act is complete. That this happens at all is further evidence that the desire for power corrupts relationships and destroys love.

In 1975, Marabel Morgan published her controversial book *The Total Woman.*[1] Some people thought that Morgan's book proposed a role for women that denied their dignity and reduced them to objects that existed solely for the sexual aggrandizement of their husbands. However, many of us in the Evangelical community realized that the book was aimed at church women who had been reared to view sex as a "wifely duty," rather than something to enjoy. For these women, Morgan's book was a liberating manifesto that freed them to improve their relationships with their mates. She declared that enjoying sex was something God intended for women as well as for men. It seems strange, some 30 years after the book was written, that there was even a question about this fact—I think most Christian women today understand that sexual gratification is a blessing from God. Yet there was a time when, as a friend of mine jokes, "we were taught that sex is a dirty, filthy thing, and you should save it for the person you marry." Marabel Morgan's ideas were liberating for women who had been brought up that way.

I do, however, still have one major objection to the book—even all these years later. I think that Morgan encouraged women to use sex in a manipulative fashion, to abandon nagging as a means of getting what they want from their husbands and resort to being sexually seductive. This, Morgan suggested, would make a husband more receptive to his wife's requests.

There can be many unintended and negative consequences of Morgan's strategy, including a husband feeling that he's been tricked and that his wife is not to be trusted. I believe that God means for sex to be used to enhance marital relationships and to enhance the humanity of the partners; when it is used as a means to control a husband, it is perverted. Christ calls Christian women to become whole, healthy persons in the context of sacrificial love; and while they should not tolerate exploitation by men, they should not play power games with their husbands either.

CHRISTIAN FEMINISM

Many Christians agree that women need to be liberated from male domination, so that they may come into the fullness of humanity God intends for them. I readily call myself a feminist and believe that both Jesus and the apostle Paul defined roles for women to establish them as equals with men. Most Christians agree that each woman possesses her own individual God-given identity and has the right to express her inherent gifts and abilities, both within the Church and within all other spheres of society.

Many claims made by secular feminists have great validity for Christians. Yet there are dangers in the women's liberation movement that are now, 40 years later, recognized by some of its most ardent supporters. There is no question that women have the right to condemn what has been done to them by 50 million aggressive, domineering, pushy husbands. However, it's obvious by now that the solution to 50 million aggressive, domineering, pushy husbands is not 50 million, aggressive, domineering, pushy wives. If the only answer to husbands who push their wives around is to teach their wives to push back, a war between the sexes is inevitable, as we've seen.

Fortunately, the Bible has a healing solution to the growing tensions sparked by the justifiable efforts of many women to affirm their dignity and worth in their marriages. The scriptural solution is to affirm the teachings of Galatians 3:28, which declares that in Christ "there is neither . . . male nor female." Because of what Christ has done and is doing in and through us, there should no longer be anything that looks like a superior/inferior relationship between men and women. God's Word declares an equality between the sexes that has been too often denied in the male-dominated Church.

The liberation of women from roles that defined them as inferior is very Christian, but women must recognize that if they are to be true followers of Christ, they must be ready to sacrifice themselves in love. In marriage, the ideal woman says to her husband, "Your dreams, your aspirations and your hopes are more important than mine. I am ready to sacrifice myself for you in love."

In response, the Christian husband should be saying, "Oh, no. You've got it all wrong! I am ready to sacrifice myself for you. I am willing to set aside my hopes, my dreams and my aspirations so that you can become the whole person God intends *you* to be."

To this, she responds, "Oh, no. It's the other way around!"—and they have their first fight. It's the only fight Christians are allowed to have. As has already been pointed out, Christians are commanded to "consider others better than yourselves" (Phil. 2:3). To be clear again: Mutual submission in love is the model for the relationship that husbands and wives should have in a Christian marriage. This is the kingdom of God's answer to the war between the sexes: We refuse to fight it.

Years ago, while hosting my early morning television show in Philadelphia, I had a guest who had authored a book destined to become "must reading" for those going through divorces. During the interview, I questioned her thesis that wives should live independently of their husbands and should not be ready to sacrifice their own personal fulfillment for the wellbeing of their children. She responded by asking, "You are not suggesting that I should sacrifice my personal fulfillment and career aspirations, along with my need for self-actualization, for my husband and children, are you?"

I replied emphatically, "Yes! There is nothing wrong with a woman sacrificing her personal aspirations, career goals and program for self-actualization to serve her husband and children. That's what marriage is all about. Nobody said you had to make those sacrifices. You could have stayed single, but since you married, you should put the wellbeing of your family above yourself. If you have a good marriage, *your husband will make the same kind of commitment*. He will put what happens to you and the children above the realization of his own personal goals and consider the self-actualization of each family member more important than anything that happens to him."

There were several letters that came to the station from the television audience, criticizing my response, but the more I think about it, the more I believe that what I said that day is true. A good marriage is a relationship in which mutual loving sacrifices are what make it work.

I know one husband who was given the opportunity for a major promotion with his employer, General Electric. The company offered him a high executive position, which would require his family to move from suburban Philadelphia to Schenectady, New York. He took the job immediately when it was offered, without talking about the move with his wife and children. He came home from work that evening, bounding into the house with news he thought would be greeted with joy. Instead, the word of his promotion created sadness and consternation. He had assumed that since the promotion was what he wanted, his wife and children should be thrilled, too. He failed to consider what the move would mean to everyone else in the family. He gave no thought to the fact that his wife would have to leave her fulfilling job and some close friends. He had no feeling for the sadness of his children who would have to leave a high school they loved. The man's daughter was a swimming star on the school team, and his son was president of the junior class; were both supposed to walk away from such things without a thought, simply because Daddy had a chance to get something he wanted?

The frustrated (and self-deceiving) father declared, "I am only doing this for the family!"

His wife responded, "Who are you kidding?"

This man was driven to reflection and to repentance, and he eventually made a decision to turn down the promotion and keep his family where they were happy. His loving sacrifice earned him incredible *authority* with his children, and they looked up to him in ways that he had hitherto seldom seen from them. Of course, his wife and children could have responded by telling him that they would gladly sacrifice themselves so that they could do what was best for him, but he never gave them the chance. He, whom male chauvinists would call "the master of the house," became the servant. All is well that ends well. Love never seeks to have its own way. It is not self-seeking (see 1 Cor. 13:5).

Ideally, the Christian family is democratic in nature. All the members see themselves as equals before God. This does not necessarily do away with the role of leadership of the father, for in a democracy there is always a leader. However, in a democracy, the leader does not function as an autocrat, but rather as an equal who is leading equals. Leadership should never be tyrannical. A Christian leader does not play power games with the family.

The Bible teaches that wherever two or three are gathered together in the name of Christ, He will be in their midst (see Matt. 18:20). This means that when family members together seek the leading of the Lord, over time they will come to a consensus. Families should pray and discuss issues until they are of one accord. It is possible to discern God's will within any body of believers that prayerfully seeks His will and waits until the Spirit creates unanimity.

Our culture does not look kindly on servanthood. But while servitude should never be forced on anyone, every Christian is called to welcome the role of a servant. No woman should be ashamed of assuming a servant role, any more than should a man. Too many times, women are made to feel that they should apologize for being "just" mothers and housewives. In reality, such roles are noble callings.

When I was on the faculty at the University of Pennsylvania, there were gatherings from time to time to which staff members were expected to bring their spouses. On one occasion, one of my female faculty colleagues confronted my wife with the question, "And what is it that *you* do, my dear?" This professor knew that my wife, Peggy, saw her primary role as raising our two children, and I believe that she may have been motivated, for her own reasons, to question the validity of Peggy's choice.

My wife, who is one of the most brilliantly articulate individuals I know, answered, "I am socializing two homo sapiens into the dominant values of the Judeo-Christian tradition in order that they might be the instruments for the transformation of the social order into the kind of teleologically prescribed utopia inherent in the eschaton!" Then Peggy asked, "And what is it that *you* do?"

My colleague answered, in a small voice, "I teach sociology."

Hurray for my wife, who understood the glory of servanthood and sacrifice for others, and the nobility of fulfilling roles that too often are diminished in our modern world!

Christ tells us that the meek shall inherit the earth (see Matt. 5:5). His message is foolishness to those committed to a lifestyle that prefers power to love. What is sad is that the most flagrant failure to understand the call of Christ to relinquish power, to discover strength in weakness and to prefer meekness and love to domination and control, often occurs among believers who claim to be followers of Christ, the ultimate Servant in human history.

Jesus leaves little room in His kingdom for male chauvinists who distort Scripture in order to legitimize their oppression of women. I am appalled by the way some men have used Scripture as a means to justify the exploitation of women—and even to legitimize abusing them.

Secular feminists have sometimes condemned the Church for, as they understand it, teaching women to put up with inferiority and domination. I truly believe that this is not the intention of most of us who stand in our churches' pulpits each week, but I wish I could say that I've never heard of a woman encouraged to submit to continued abuse.

I am the patron of a ministry in the northeast of England called Aquila Way, which has an extensive ministry to abused women. It is horrible how prevalent is the belief among these women that the abuse received at the hands of their husbands was something they ought not to have opposed. On one occasion, a woman told me that she had returned to the home where she was physically abused—on the recommendation of her pastor! He taught a gross misinterpretation of biblical submission, and it nearly cost her life.

As horrifying as physical abuse is, we must recognize that verbal abuse can sometimes do as much, or even more, damage than physical violence. That old saying—the one about sticks and stones breaking bones but words never hurting—is a lie. No woman should be the target of hateful words, hurtful blows or humiliating sex, and anyone (including a pastor) who says otherwise is dead wrong.

There are Christian feminists such as Mary Stewart Van Leeuwen, a colleague of mine at Eastern University, who are powerful advocates for women's equality within the parameters of Scripture. She offers convincing biblical support for the claim that Jesus opposed any form of second-class citizenship for women, and has developed a major course of study on feminist issues from a Christian perspective. Courses of study such as she offers should be required for both men and women in Christian universities and colleges.

It was Evangelicalism in the 1800s that gave birth to the women's suffrage movement. Charles Finney, the acknowledged "Billy Graham" of the nineteenth century, made women's suffrage a major part of his evangelistic preaching. When Finney invited people to accept Christ, he simultaneously asked them if they would join either the anti-slave movement or the women's suffrage movement; he believed that those were the two dominant movements through which God was working in that day. The modern feminist movement began in churches in the upper part of New York State, largely under the influence of Evangelical revivalism. Often, radical feminists have regarded religion to be oppressive so far as women's rights are concerned. The truth is that the Church has a long way to go, but we were in on the ground floor!

Jesus once and for all changed the status of women by treating them as equals. He invited women to be students of the Torah, which back then was a privilege reserved only for men (see Luke 10:38-42). He broke the religious taboo on touching women when they were menstruating (see Mark 5:25-30). He was even willing to transgress ancient Jewish standards of social respectability by establishing relationships with women of questionable ethnic and moral backgrounds (see John 4:1-27).

If we claim to follow Jesus, shouldn't Christian men be as daring in our respect for and elevation of women? The greatest hurdle for biblical equality is not how women can gain power—though in some instances they need to do just that—but how men can relinquish power. The gospel stands in opposition to any teaching that encourages men to oppress women. Instead, ours is a gospel that calls upon men to yield their power in order to express love.

WOMEN IN THE CHURCH

I am convinced that women are called into all roles in the life of the Church, including the role of preacher. I believe that Christians should condemn the denial of called and anointed women into these roles—a practice that oppresses women and hurts the Church. I make this claim based on the fact that, in the New Testament, we find women occupying high offices in the early Church, setting models for contemporary Church life. For instance, a woman held the role of apostle, the highest office in the Church. We read in Romans 16:7 that Junia, a woman, was an apostle. And that's not the only place in Scripture where we find women exercising key roles of leadership in the Church. In the book of Acts, we find that Philip had three daughters who were preachers (another name for *prophet* in the Greek language; see Acts 21:8-9), and that Euodias and Syntyche were strong leaders in the early Church (see Phil. 4:2). When spiritual gifts, such as preaching, were received and recognized in the early Church, there is no indication that only men were given these gifts (see Eph. 4:11-12).

I have always found it perplexing that male-dominated churches that have kept women from becoming pastors and preachers have generally been more than ready to send women as missionaries to foreign fields. As a case in point, the Southern Baptist Convention, which does not allow women to occupy the role of preacher, has, over the years, sent thousands of dedicated women to overseas mission fields in places such as Africa, Asia and Latin America. As a matter of fact, one of their foremost missionary saints is Lotti Moon, a woman whom they honor each year by calling Southern Baptist churches to take up a special offering for missionary work in her honor. It's not outrageous to ask if there might be some subtle racism in all of this, in that it suggests white women can preach to men of color but not to white men. Or perhaps it is okay for women to preach in dangerous overseas situations, as long as they don't threaten to usurp the pulpits right here in North America, which we men believe are ordained only for men? It's all very confusing to me.

I believe that in the family, in the Church and in society at large, women should be free to exercise their gifts—the Holy Spirit has provided those gifts for them and for the benefit of the Church. In the name of Christ, inferior status for women should be smashed and women should be liberated in order that they might freely live out sacrificial service in the home, in the Church and in the workplace—and wherever else God calls them to be. But even as they take on roles hitherto reserved exclusively for men, women must avoid the pitfalls that those who hold positions of power often fall into, with destructive consequences.

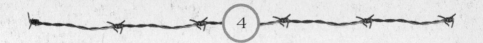

WHEN CHILDREN
GET POWER

Power struggles within the family are not confined to the relationship between husbands and wives. Increasingly, children have gotten into the fray, and many parents find their offspring painfully confrontational, asserting themselves against parental authority.

The old adage that "children should be seen and not heard" belongs to another era. Things are different nowadays. Nothing has changed the traditionally prescribed role for children as much as the transition in the West from a rural, agrarian society to being an urban, industrial society.

In a farm society, all the members of the family work in the same place. Children work in the fields alongside their fathers and mothers. This places fathers in a situation wherein they can control what goes on in the lives of family members. In short, an agrarian society is very oriented toward creating a male-dominated family. But this orientation changed when America ceased being an agrarian society. In 1900, 20 percent of Americans lived on farms. Today, that number is less than 4 percent.[1]

In our modern, urban, industrial society, fathers usually work away from their homes in offices and factories. Fathers, for the most part, are no longer the ones who exercise discipline when children step out of line—they are not there to do so. Given the absence of fathers, it would seem natural for mothers to take over leadership roles and become the disciplinarians. But in many American homes, mothers have not assumed this role. That is because mothers have been victimized by what I call the "Cult of Mom-ism." From a host of sources, mothers have been told that their primary function is to be objects of love. From Freudian psychology and Dr. Spock, they have learned that being loved by their children is the determining factor for healthy early childhood development. Magazines like *Redbook*, *Woman's Day* and *Ladies Home Journal* have carried countless articles that have popularized this view, and daytime television talk shows such as *Oprah* and *Dr. Phil* have communicated it so widely that it has become a culturally accepted truism.

While I strongly affirm the belief that mothers should unconditionally love their children, I think it is a mistake to over-emphasize their role as love objects to the point that mothers are intimidated by children who threaten to withhold their love unless they get what they want. Mothers have gotten the message that their children are supposed to love them intensely at all times, and it is difficult for any mother to provide, in her husband's absence, the kind of leadership children need if she feels that her children must be always warmly disposed toward her. In the old days, mother and father could work as a team, with father assuming the role of disciplinarian. Now the father is gone from the home from morning until night, and many mothers are afraid to exercise strong leadership and discipline because they fear incurring resentment from their children.

If the father cannot lead because he is absent from the household, and the mother is afraid to exercise leadership for fear of incurring resentment from her children, it is easy to see how we have become a culture in which children dominate their families. For the first time in history, the filiocentric, or child-centered, family has become normative. Children often seem to rule in American families.

If you're not convinced, go to a supermarket and watch the interactions between some children and their mothers. Time and time again, you will see mothers giving in to their children's demands. The children seem to get their way simply by threatening their mothers with temper tantrums. In short, children appear to know that by communicating a threat that they might no longer love their mothers, they exercise power.

I want to ward off any suggestion that raising children should be a role prescribed for mothers only. I believe, as do many of my fellow Christian sociologists, that raising children should be a bi-parental responsibility. It would be ideal if every couple could arrange things as one Christian couple I know has done: Both husband and wife have part-time jobs and they schedule themselves so that each spends an almost equal amount of time raising their children. It's an ideal that is seldom possible, but it is still one that I think should be held up as an example. Men should not be denied the joys that come from nurturing infants through childhood. Given the normative realities of life in today's world, wherein fathers are away from their children for the better part of most days, special efforts should be made to involve dads as much as possible in the rearing of their children.

INSECURE PARENTS AND WILLFUL CHILDREN

Back in the early days of my preaching, I had a sermon titled "Ten Commandments for Raising Children." But, after marrying and becoming a father of two children, I changed the title of that sermon to "Ten *Suggestions* for Raising Children." As I struggled with my son and daughter through their tumultuous teenage years, I had an inclination to change the sermon title one more time to read "Ten *Hints* for Raising Children." Raising children has always presented challenges, but in the context of America's rapid transition into a modern, urban, industrial society, with its changing roles for mothers and fathers, it has been hard to figure out just how families should function without giving in to the power plays of children.

It is simple to recognize the problem, but it is difficult to supply an answer. Even children who are not raised in an overly permissive manner may assert themselves against parental authority. It is not unusual for a child raised in the Church and provided with solid guidelines for life to become openly defiant of his or her parents. To make matters worse, some unthinking church member might offhandedly quip, "Train up a child in the way he should go, and when he is old he will not depart from it" (Prov. 22:6). Usually anyone who so readily quotes that verse does not have any children. Parents know that rearing children is just not that simple in the modern world.

These days, a child's training comes from a multitude of sources, in addition to his parents. School, peers, neighbors and media all communicate values and lifestyles to children growing up in America. Often these messages from outside sources are diametrically opposed to what parents are trying to instill in their children. Compared with these alternate agents of socialization, parents often appear naïve and out of date.

Children are not Pavlovian dogs who simply act as they have been trained to behave. We all know parents who have brought up their children "right" only to have them disastrously rebel. What is even more perplexing is that we also know of others who break every prescription for parenting, but nevertheless end up with model children. Face it! Children have wills of their own. They can easily be tempted to seek the power to control their own lives in accord with influences that come from outside the home. Sometimes parents are able to mold their wills, but in other cases, parental toughness only results in children becoming more defiant.

WHEN PARENTS MUST USE POWER

When I was a boy, my father punished me. He said what many fathers say to their children: "This is going to hurt me more than it will hurt you." As he paddled my rear end, I found that very hard to believe.

Time has passed, and from my own experience as a father, I can assure you that my father was right. Punishing children must be the most difficult part of parenting; yet at times it is necessary. (Unlike my father, I never utilized corporal punishment on either of my children. As a sociologist, I knew that corporal punishment often fosters abusive behavior when those children come of age and are married and have children of their own. But punishment was still a facet of my parenting approach!)

Parents want their children to voluntarily do what is good; they do not want to force their children to be obedient. They want their children to do what is right because they are motivated by love and reason, rather than by threats of punishment. Whenever a child is punished, particularly when that punishment is corporal in nature, the parents experience a sense of failure. They inwardly say, "This shouldn't be necessary."

The parents of one teenager who was arrested on a drug use charge said over and over again, "How could he do this after we loved him so much?" They viewed their son's wrong behavior as evidence of his rejection of their love. They had found a large supply of marijuana cigarettes in his room and also discovered a significant quantity of cocaine. Upon investigation, they learned that their son had been selling drugs to his friends to earn money to pay for his own drug habit. When they realized what had happened in their son's life, they decided to turn him over to the police.

It was with deep regret that they resorted to the use of force to correct their son. As they did so, there was a tremendous sense of failure on their part. Nevertheless, they knew that punishment was necessary and that they had to use force to direct their son to do what was right.

Children, long before they should be, are tempted to establish themselves as adults by seeking power. They want to be in charge of their lives. They want to be able to decide for themselves what they will do and when they will do it. They do not want other people, especially their parents, telling them what they can and cannot do. Consequently, children often defy their parents, testing them, to see what they can get away with.

Sometimes parents yield to their children's claims on independence and power, only to find that their children are not happy with the power they have gained. This, I believe, is because children are somewhat ambivalent about power.

On the one hand, they are tempted to secure it—after all, children are human too, driven by the "will to power." If this temptation is not checked, they tend to dominate their parents. We have all witnessed situations in which children have gained such control over their families.

On the other hand, children feel insecure when they are able to dominate their parents. They lose confidence in their parents and become afraid of being in charge. They realize that their freedom from their parents' directives leaves them with the burden of deciding for themselves what is best and what will make them happy. They are not sure that they are up to handling the decision-making processes that are thrust upon them. In such situations, children are relieved when parents reestablish control, even if it means that their parents have to resort to punishment to do so.

I remember times when my children in their early years tried to assert themselves and take charge of their lives. They would do this by trying to defy my wishes and the wishes of my wife. They would resist doing what they were told. My wife, who was the more compassionate between the two of us, would endeavor to reason with them and show them through long drawn-out explanations why it would be best for them to do what they were told. These discussions would often go on and on, with the children becoming more and more agitated.

The mistake was to think that our children were simply confused and needed clarification, and that all that was necessary was to show them why what we were asking was best for them. But this talking seldom worked. We had to assert ourselves and, if necessary, even use punishment. Much to our surprise and relief, the children often calmed down immediately when the rules were reestablished and punishment was exercised. They actually seemed happier—and, in reality, they were. When control was taken away from them, they were relieved.

My wife and I never really felt good about punishing our children, but there were times when we found it necessary. We wished that they would simply be obedient out of love, but in the absence of loving obedience we had to exercise power.

Every child will press to determine the limits of his or her power, and if no limits are set, that child will press further and further until he or she seems incorrigible. That child must be stopped from pursuing such self-destructive behavior, and sometimes parents must resort to power in order to establish what is best for him or her. The child may not want to brush her teeth, or go to bed at the proper time, or go to school. Obviously, the child must be required to do what she may not want to do.

There have been times when parents have come to me for counseling and asked, "What if my child does not want to go to church? If I force my child to go, won't I contribute to having my child hate church and never want to go again?"

What such parents need to realize is that the child may not so much be rebelling against church as rebelling against them. The child may be testing the parents' willingness to stand up to his demands, exploring the extent of his powers. How resolved are the parents? This is the real question such tests are asking. In such a case, yielding to the child's demands is to encourage further challenges to the parents' authority.

Every child is born with the same will to power that has marked humanity from the time of Adam and Eve. Each one wants to assert his or her will. Consequently, there is a rebellious spirit that lurks inside even the most compliant of children, and that rebellious spirit must, at times, be challenged by the parents' use of power. This loving exercise of power is occasionally necessary, and no one should feel guilty when it is required.

Some years ago, while lecturing at the University of Pennsylvania, I was talking about what could be done to control destructively willful children. In the course of my lecture, I pointed out that I did not believe in corporal punishment. I introduced the students to several empirical studies that found a strong relationship between childhood corporal punishment and adulthood abuse. I proposed that striking a child as a form of punishment is unnecessary and likely harmful. My students immediately questioned my assertion and created all kinds of scenarios wherein physical punishment might be the only alternative. Finally, I capitulated and said, "Okay! There may be a rare instance where corporal punishment may be the only means of dealing with the situation, but you should never strike a child in anger."

The next day, one of the students stood before the lecture of the day began and said, "I have a little poem in honor of yesterday's pronouncement by the professor concerning corporal punishment." He read:

Never strike a child in anger!
Never hit him when irate!
Save it for some happy time,
When both are feeling great.

Needless to say, those lines elicited a great deal of laughter—but my point cannot be taken lightly. There are effective ways of punishing children *without* resorting to corporal means. Withholding privileges and limiting activities (that is, grounding) are particularly effective methods for teenagers who value their freedoms and independence. For a younger child, requiring a quiet time or "time out," when he or she must be absolutely still and silent for up to 10 minutes, is a valuable punishment. Its effect is twofold: first, the child has time to think about his or her wrongdoing and what he or she should do differently next time; and second, a few minutes of peace can help his or her energy level come down to manageable levels.

PARENTING BY THE BOOK

When a child comes eventually to recognize the Bible as the ultimate authority for behavior, disciplinary problems may be well on their way to being solved. In order for this to happen, the parents must let the child know from his or her earliest days that the Bible is the ultimate source of authority over all they do as parents and over how they expect her to behave. When a child realizes that parents are not arbitrary rulers, but are themselves obedient to a higher law, it encourages viewing Scripture as deserving of ultimate respect. Parents should help a child see that what they require is in accord with the teachings of Scripture. This is a lot better than demanding obedience and telling their child to obey simply "because I said so!" Whenever possible, parents should be ready to show that what they ask is in accord with God's will and God's Word.

It is obvious that parents cannot come up with a verse for every situation in life, but they should try to explain the basic principles of right and wrong as set forth in the Bible, and show then how the rules they have established are in accord with those principles. (Obviously, this will require more Bible study on the part of parents than is now typically the case.) Whenever parents lay down the rules and requirements for behavior, bright children can be expected to respond by asking, "Why?" They are seeking reasons and parents should be prepared to relate through reason or the Scriptures why their children are expected to behave.

When the Bible says, "Children, obey your parents *in the Lord*" (Eph. 6:1, emphasis added), it is making a very important point, but children will not accede to biblical authority unless they know that their parents are also submissive to that same authority. If you read on in that chapter of Ephesians, you will discover that there are also requisites for parents. They are warned not to "exasperate your children" (Eph. 6:4), which can be done by overcorrecting them.

Only parents who are not afraid of losing power are capable of having an honest relationship with their children. For instance, when a child is the victim of a parent's wrongdoing, the parent should ask the child for forgiveness. Unfortunately, many parents are reluctant to do this. They are anxious to preserve an image of infallibility and omnipotence with their children, driven by a fear that confessing their failures would hurt that image. Consequently, they maintain a façade of having done nothing wrong, even when this is not the case. Children learn from their parents, and if the parents never admit that they have done wrong, then children will also be incapable of admitting failure—even when it's obvious that they have failed to do the right thing. This inability may ultimately affect the ability of these children to become Christians. Having been conditioned never to confess faults or ask for forgiveness, such children may find it impossible to confess their sins to God and ask for God's forgiveness. Playing the power game can ultimately separate children from the love of God! Such is the price to be paid when we are afraid to give up power.

Another disturbing development in family relationships has resulted from the growth of professionalism in the rearing of children. Since the time of the child psychologist Henry Stack Sullivan, there has been an increasing sense that professional help from social scientists is needed to properly socialize children into adulthood. Parents have been led to doubt their own ability to successfully rear their sons and daughters. Sociologists, psychologists and social workers have often left parents with the impression that only experts who have been specially trained for the task possess the techniques essential for the rearing of children. They have implied, through their work, that most parents do not know enough to parent effectively. Accordingly, there have been some social scientists who have suggested that child-rearing should be professionalized. Perplexed parents, given such judgments from the "experts," become all too ready to turn over their children to daycare programs and nursery schools staffed by trained personnel.

I am not suggesting that nursery schools for children are a bad idea. In America, where nearly 35-percent of children are living in single-parent families,[2] nursery schools have become absolutely essential for mothers who must work outside their homes. Not for one moment am I opposed to nursery schools in such situations, but I have to wonder why parents would want to turn a child over to a nursery school for rearing if they don't have to. I ask, "Don't you want to be there when your child says his or her first words? Don't you want to enjoy those moments when you watch that boy or girl gain the growing awareness of the joys of the surrounding world? Don't you want to be the one who communicates Christian values to your children, especially in light of the fact that 'the professionals' indicate that values and beliefs are instilled in the earliest years of child development?"

I do not agree that the social scientists are the experts who know what is best for children. Studies validate that most parents do a pretty decent job of child-rearing and instinctively know what is best for their child. Those who have raised more than one child know that the techniques effectively employed for one might not work for another. Children are different and need to be raised differently and, from my observation, parents are the best ones to have a "feel" for what is best for each of their children.

This is not to call into question the good advice and information that can come from social scientists, but only to affirm that parents, in spite of any academic shortcomings regarding the child-rearing processes, can still be counted on in most cases—not all—to know what is best for their children. Children need leadership in the household, and insofar as mothers and fathers support each other in their parenting roles, they will be able to prevent children from playing power games and asserting themselves in destructive patterns—often without help from the "experts."

POWER GAMES WITH TEENAGERS

People from other cultures often remark that American young people seem out of control and disrespectful of their parents. What these outside observers usually fail to realize is that a major cause of the decline of parental authority in our society is, in part, due to rapidly changing norms for teenagers, resulting from unstoppable social changes. In America and the West, parents have to deal with living in a technological milieu that makes traditional customs dysfunctional and outmoded. Our world is changing so quickly under the impact of technology that many parents are confused about what they should expect from their adolescent children. When they endeavor to direct the lives of their teenage children by telling them what they can and cannot do, they cannot appeal to tradition and say, "This is the way it has always been done." They, as well as their teenaged children, know that in this "brave new world," the traditional rules do not apply.

In a society made shaky because of collapsing institutions in our chaotic society, children are likely to make the expectations of their peer groups the determiners of their behavior. Parents are often challenged with, "but all the other kids are doing it." Insecure parents, not knowing what is normative for teenagers and afraid to force their children into a lifestyle that might make them socially unacceptable to their friends, often give in to such pressure, allowing children who are coming of age to gain significant power to self-determine what they can and cannot do.

It is easy to demonstrate the destructive effects of possessing such power as we study the effect on children. Erik Erikson, one of the early figures in the field of human development, noted that children become emotionally disturbed when they are forced to assume the power to exercise responsibilities that they are not mature enough to handle. For instance, if children at the age of 12 are given the power to exercise privileges that should be given to young people in their middle or late teens, they become frustrated and disoriented. They can, when this happens, become emotionally disturbed.[3]

We see this kind of emotional disturbance running rampant in our world today. Parents allow their children to grow up far too quickly. Not sure of themselves as parents, they give in to their children's demands for privileges and rights that their children are not yet ready to handle. In many cases, kids in their early teens become confused and angry as they find themselves with the power to make decisions they are unprepared to make. Adolescents need restraints and enforced rules. If their lives do not have order, children are likely to become depressed. Then parents often are at a loss to understand the depression and sadness in their teen-aged children. They say, "We've given them everything they want, yet they're unhappy." It seldom occurs to them that their children are unhappy *because* they've gotten everything they want.

Émile Durkheim, considered by many to be one of the fathers of sociology, discovered that without clearly defined norms and rules to govern life, people become self-destructive and even suicidal. A state of normlessness, which Durkheim called "anomie," is responsible for the depression that can drive young people to drug use, alcoholism and delinquency.[4] Given the normlessness that marks the lives of so many American teenagers, Durkheim would not be surprised at the prevalence of drug use and alcoholism in American high schools. Lack of regulation in the lives of contemporary youth has become a major source of the destructive problems that emotionally cripple so many young people.

Defiance of parental authority has become a hallmark of our times. More and more parents complain about their inability to control their teenagers. Many of them realize their teens are more influenced by the crowd they run with than by the teachings they receive at home or at church. Parental efforts to enforce rules and regulations are often greeted with open defiance. This creates such hurt and dismay that a surprising number of parents admit that if they had it to do over again, they would not have any children.

This may sound like an overstatement, but it is not: Parental failure to establish boundaries for their child's behavior can destroy their teen's ability to love. Parents often feel that their teenaged children do not love them, and sadly, it's not just their imagination. There are children who have little concern for the feelings of their parents. Again we see that as power increases, love decreases. Young people who have been given too much power are usually extremely unhappy and malcontented. They have gained power, but what they have lost is infinitely more precious.

It is important for parents to define for their adolescent children what is expected of them in the years ahead. A study of Japanese mothers found that when they were asked, "What do you want your children to be when they grow up?" they answered, "We want our children to be *successful*."[5] This may explain why the Japanese are considered such a "driven" people: Children are raised to strive for success and to make any sacrifice that achievements require. Japanese children and teenagers, on average, study longer and work harder in school than do their American counterparts. As adults, they tend to live success-oriented lives.

When American mothers were asked exactly the same question, they responded, "We want our children to be *happy*."[6] There is a line in the Declaration of Independence that every American knows by heart: Every person is entitled to "life, liberty and the pursuit of happiness." Of course, happiness is important, but those who are wise know that happiness is a by-product, not a goal in and of itself; it is gained when one is focused on worthier pursuits. We should pray for God to help us to rescue teenagers from the consequences of making the pursuit of happiness their ultimate goal.

It is no wonder that, in adulthood, many of these children have unsuccessful marriages—they evaluate everything in terms of whether or not it makes them happy. There are times in the vast majority of marriages when the people involved aren't particularly happy, and unless they have reasons other than happiness to stay together through those difficult times, their marriages are likely to end in divorce.

When I was a boy growing up in an old-fashioned Italian family, my mother and father had a different answer to the question, "What do you want your son to be when he grows up?" Both of them would have said, "I want my son to be *good!*" The Bible calls on us to recognize that it's not happiness that should follow us all the days of our lives; it should be "goodness and mercy" (see Ps. 24). My parents exercised the kinds of controls that sometimes kept me from doing what I thought would make me happy because they were committed to making me into a good person.

Something that can significantly contribute to delivering a family with teenagers from chaotic normlessness is to establish—through discussion, prayer and Bible study—a sense of family mission. Stephen B. Covey, the well-known guru in the field of organizational management, has proposed that every family hammer out a mission statement that clearly states what their family is all about, and what goals define their life as a family.[7]

In retrospect, I see that when I was coming of age, my family did just that. It was not as though any particular meetings were called to specify the mission of our family, but there emerged, largely through informal discussions around the dinner table, that our family was committed to doing God's work in the world. The Church was viewed as the instrument of God through which we could work to change the world into the kind of world God created it to be. Primary in these efforts were two things: winning people to a faith commitment to Christ, and ministering to the needs of the poor and the oppressed. From my earliest days, I knew that each of us in the Campolo family were expected to live out our lives sacrificially for the sake of Christ and His kingdom. This commitment, in my case, carried with it behavioral expectations established through rules and regulations. Our lives were circumscribed by our sense of mission and we were not free to do whatever we wanted to do.

Looking back, I realize that I was socialized into the legalistic traditions of an Evangelical-fundamentalist subculture that we were convinced was God-ordained. There are those who speak disparagingly of such a fundamentalist upbringing, but not me. It is easy to see, looking back on my early years, that rules for what I could and could not do saved me from a normless, disorganized life of the kind all too evident in our fragmented and confused Western world. Those rules and regulations, absorbed into my thinking without question, carried me through my teenage years with a sense of security and wellbeing. My life, as I came of age, was in marked contrast to the tumultuous strivings of so many young people I encounter these days.

Fundamentalism, with its rules and regulations that are now viewed as more like tribal rituals than biblically based principles, was for me a necessary stage in my development. It is a stage that I hope all Christians outgrow as they seek for well-thought-out reasons for what they do (see 1 Pet. 3:15). But it takes time and much maturing to reach that point, and teenagers usually are not yet able to pull that off effectively. I feel sorry for those who never had prescribed rules and regulations to reign in their whims and wishes, but I also feel sorry for those who do not outgrow them and come to define for themselves, in the context of biblical reflection, principles to live by.

In the context of ongoing family discussions—an increasing rarity in our helter-skelter, rushed lifestyles—parents must enable their teenagers to learn, think, question and explore the guiding rules for living and help them establish within the family's defined mission a sense of what they should do with their lives.

Purpose cannot be imposed by powerful parents without the possibility of resentments and rebellion. But such conflict can be creative—a part of what sociologists call a "dialectical process." That academic phrase simply means that out of conflict can come some really wonderful results. The mission of the family becomes what we call the "thesis" of the dialectical process. Emerging out of the thesis, and in conflict with it, there can be an anti-thesis. In the context of a family, this anti-thesis may be the individual teenager asserting personal will and individuality. But out of the conflict between the thesis (family mission) and the anti-thesis (the teen's will), there can eventually emerge a synthesis that sheds some traits of both the thesis and the anti-thesis and brings together the best elements of both.

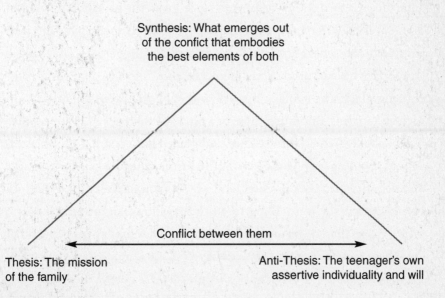

Synthesis: What emerges out of the confict that embodies the best elements of both

Conflict between them

Thesis: The mission of the family

Anti-Thesis: The teenager's own assertive individuality and will

Only a power-hungry parent would want a teenager to be a cookie-cutter replica of himself or herself—every person is created uniquely by God. On the other hand, teens should not be abandoned to just do their own thing, formulating their values and priorities without guidance from their parents. A child should come to maturity under the influence of the values, lifestyle and commitments inherent in the family's mission, allowed to express his individuality, creativity and a special calling from God. This balance is what I mean by "the synthesis."

Above all, parents must exercise patience and pray. A lot. It is surprising to many parents how their young adult children come around eventually to being the ideal persons they hoped their teens would become. Parents should never give up believing that something good can happen, even when it seems as though all hope might as well be abandoned. Let me tell you about an extreme situation in which it seemed that all hope was lost.

Once I was speaking at a chapel service at a Christian university and noticed that, seated on the front row, were a couple of middle-aged parents. They seemed somewhat out of place, given the youthful makeup of the audience. Afterward, these parents wanted to speak with me, and they told me a heartbreaking, yet heartwarming, story. They had a daughter who had been incredibly rebellious. She had dressed "Goth," wearing black attire, black lipstick and sporting extensive tattoos on each of her arms. But much more of a problem than her edgy appearance was her belligerent attitude. They had prayed long and hard for her salvation, pleading with God to change her from a person filled with anger and defiance into the daughter God would want her to be. She had told her folks that she was willing to go to this Christian university for no other reason than to get away from them—she despised them that much!

These parents were most anxious to tell me that a year earlier, when I had been at this same school and preached a gospel message, their daughter had responded by giving her life to Christ. After having made this life-altering decision, their daughter had gone back to her dormitory to write a gracious and loving letter to her parents. In that letter, she had begged for forgiveness for all the hurt she had inflicted on them. She explained that she had had an experience with the Holy Spirit that surely would make her into a new kind of person. She couldn't wait until she could get home to let her parents hug her as they had always wanted to, and she was looking forward to how good things would be in their family from this point on. The letter went on and on with such beautiful sentiments.

After mailing the letter in the nearby town, tragedy struck. On the way back to her dormitory, their daughter was in a horrendous automobile accident and was killed.

These parents buried their daughter with broken hearts. They despaired over how their relationship with her had ended without reconciliation and healing. But three days after the funeral, a seeming miracle happened. The precious letter written by their daughter arrived in the mail.

I foolishly said, "It's such a shame that the letter came too late."

The parents answered, "It wasn't too late! There will be a time when she *will* hug us and we *will* hug her, just as she hoped when she wrote those beautiful words."

God has a way of bringing hope out of despair! Just when it seems "it's over," God brings a new beginning.

RELINQUISHING POWER

Parents must be very careful about how they wield their power, lest they become too restrictive and exercise a destructive influence in the lives of their children. Controlling young adults after they reach an age when they should begin to practice controlling themselves can encourage an unhealthy dependency. By constantly doing for their children what they can do for themselves, parents maintain unhealthy power over them and retard their growth into maturity.

During my teaching days at Eastern University, I observed a young woman who was kept under the domination of her parents throughout her college career. Her parents came to visit her every weekend, interrupting the time she might have spent having fun and developing healthy relationships with other students. They gave their daughter everything she needed or requested. They constantly interfered in situations she should have handled herself. If she had problems in a particular course, her parents called on the professor to discuss the problems. If she had difficulty with her roommate, they complained to the dean of students. By constantly doing for their daughter what she should have been doing herself, they prevented her from ever growing up. Staying under their control, she never became independent. She never married. So far as I know, they still take care of her.

These parents would claim that they love their daughter, but they do not love her enough to let her go. They do not love her enough to relinquish their power over her. They so much enjoy having her under their control that they have stunted her actualization into the fulfilled person God intends her to be.

Parents must learn to relinquish control over their children. Love requires it. Sometimes it is painful for parents to stand by and watch their children do things they know are self-defeating and hurtful, but loving parents are ready to endure that suffering rather than interfere with their children in ways that keep them from growing up.

RELIGIOUS POWER PLAYS

The apostle Paul was concerned about a power struggle going on between Euodia and Syntyche, two leaders of the Philippian church. Their struggle was, in part, his motivation for writing his letter to the Philippians. As far as we know, these two women had been coworkers with Paul in establishing the Christian work in Philippi. Unfortunately, Euodia and Syntyche had since been seduced into playing power games. Each was struggling for a dominant position within the church. Each gathered a group of supporters and, in the power struggle that followed, there was every possibility that the church at Philippi would go through a schism.

In his letter, Paul pleaded with Euodia and Syntyche to be "like-minded" with one another. More specifically, he wanted them to imitate Christ by abandoning their quests for power and domination. He urged everyone in the Philippian congregation, and especially Euodia and Syntyche, to work for harmony and to give up playing power games. Paul wrote:

Make my joy complete by being like-minded, having the same love, being one in spirit and purpose. Do nothing out of selfish ambition or vain conceit, but in humility consider others better than yourselves (Phil. 2:2-3).

Paul urged the entire church to use Christ as their model:

Your attitude should be the same as that of Christ Jesus: Who, being in very nature God, did not consider equality with God something to be grasped, but made himself nothing, taking the very nature of a servant, being made in human likeness. And being found in appearance as a man, he humbled himself and became obedient to death—even death on a cross! (Phil. 2:5-8).

Paul pointed out that Christ set aside His power when He entered into history as a man. In these verses, he told Euodia and Syntyche that Jesus became an obedient Servant, willing to humble Himself for the sake of others, and that Paul expected them to imitate their Lord. Jesus did not come as a ruling monarch. Instead, Paul declared, He chose to be a suffering Servant, willing to surrender Himself to death on the cross. Paul contrasted Jesus' approach to the power seeking of Euodia and Syntyche. Jesus was willing to set aside power to sacrificially express His love, while Euodia and Syntyche, on the other hand, had set aside love to engage in a power struggle. Paul called on them to change.

From the earliest days of Christianity to the present the Church has continued to be threatened by power plays. Sometimes its members are jealous of the power of the pastor and work to undermine him or her. In more cases than I care to number, church members have even sought to "break" a pastor and bring him or her under their control. Such power plays can take a variety of forms, but the most common is an attempt to weaken the pastor through constant criticism. Instead of praying for their pastor, they prey on the preacher, picking on every little fault they can find. They may even ridicule the pastor to other church members in their attempts to diminish his or her authority in the eyes of the rest of the congregation.

When I was a young pastor, there was a woman in my church who was out to get me. She criticized the way I preached, the way I dressed and the way I greeted people after the Sunday worship service. Demonstrating the ludicrous extremes to which she was willing to go, she claimed that during the celebration of Holy Communion, I ate my bread too quickly. She actually brought that up at a church business meeting! This woman had intimidated and dominated the former pastor and was trying to do the same with me.

I did not help the situation with my determination to show her she could not push me around. In my own power play, I went out of my way to prove that I was in control of the church and that she could not stop me. Between the two of us, the church suffered greatly. I should have known better and acted differently.

In most cases, members who struggle to gain control of a church are people who have a sense of powerlessness in their everyday lives. Perhaps they feel put down at their jobs or find themselves dominated at home. In one way or another, these members are usually persons who feel diminished by others, and find that within the church they can get away with asserting themselves or even being aggressive. They discover that the church provides them with opportunities to dominate, as a way to compensate for their sense of powerlessness in the outside world. Most churches are so desperate to maintain the support of their members that it is easy for such power-hungry individuals to manipulate this dependence into an opportunity for power games. This is particularly true in small churches, where a single family leaving the congregation can be disastrous for the financial support of the church. By threatening to withhold financial support or to leave the church, power-playing members can pressure the pastor to comply with their wishes. In a small church, the simple threat not to attend services can blackmail a pastor into yielding.

When I was a pastor, I often wished I had a thousand members in my congregation, just so that I could be indifferent to similar threats. I wanted to be the pastor of a church so large that people would know their absence wouldn't even be noticed. Being immature, I did not know how to react in a Christ-like love to threats and wished for the *power* of a large congregation.

St. Paul faced up to challenges to his authority from people who wanted to replace him in the leadership of the Church. Some questioned his qualifications; others questioned his spirituality; still others raised doubts about his zeal. Paul answered his detractors by claiming that, by any outward measure, he was qualified. He wrote:

> I myself have reasons for such confidence. If anyone else thinks he has reasons to put confidence in the flesh, I have more: circumcised on the eighth day, of the people of Israel, of the tribe of Benjamin, a Hebrew of Hebrews; in regard to the law, a Pharisee; as for zeal, persecuting the church; as for legalistic righteousness, faultless (Phil. 3:4-6).

Paul did not believe, however, that these worldly achievements were of any great significance. Instead, he dismissed his list of credentials as having little or no value, making it clear that the only thing that really mattered was his submission to Jesus. He wrote in Philippians 3:7, "But whatever was to my profit I now consider loss for the sake of Christ."

Paul based his authority on how much he had suffered for Christ. He contended that in seeking the role of a suffering servant, rather than that of a powerbroker or officeholder, he had established himself as the kind of leader modeled after Christ.

Paul made it clear that within the Church, people should seek to humbly serve each other, rather than to rule over each other. He wrote in Galatians 6:2 that Christians should be ready to bear one another's burdens in order to fulfill the law of Christ. He criticized all power struggles in the Church and allowed for only one kind of competition: to "outdo one another in love" (Rom. 12:10, *RSV*). He encouraged church members to put others above themselves and to render service to others.

ATTEMPTS TO MANIPULATE GOD

Some church members think that they can play power games with God, manipulating the Creator of the universe into a state of obligation. They believe that if they do enough good works, God will owe them blessings in this life and salvation in the life to come. They can't get it through their heads that salvation is given to those who know they have no power to obtain it for themselves. As many times as they may have heard it, they still don't get it. *We are saved by grace, not by works!* Salvation is a gift! No one can boast that he or she has earned it. That's what it says in the Scriptures:

> For it is by grace you have been saved, through faith—and this
> not from yourselves, it is the gift of God—not by works, so that
> no one can boast (Eph. 2:8-9).

People who are in love with power cannot handle this. They want to establish qualifications for eternal life through their own efforts, but we are saved by rendering ourselves helpless before God and by allowing God to do what we are unable to do for ourselves. Jesus saves those who acknowledge that they come to Him in weakness. Those who think they have the power to earn salvation through good works are in for a surprise on Judgment Day.

I am increasingly concerned that so many people play manipulative games with God. They make their religion into an attempt to get what they want from the "Great Vending Machine in the Sky." We see this most clearly in what is known as the "prosperity gospel." This, however, is not religion. It is magic disguised as religion.

Bronislaw Malinowski, one of the great anthropologists of the twentieth century, differentiated between magic and religion.[1] Magic, as he defined it, is a system in which people endeavor to gain control over spiritual forces in order that they might obtain from them what they desire. It is a means of gaining power to dictate what spiritual forces give. In contrast, claimed Malinowski, religion is a system wherein people surrender themselves to spiritual forces, becoming servants through whom those spiritual forces can work out divine purposes in the world.

According to Malinowski's definitions, there is a great deal of magic going on in many churches these days, passing itself off as true religion. Many people are looking for just the right formula to get their prayers answered. It's so tempting to try to bargain with God; to treat God as some kind of transcendental Santa Claus in the sky who will give us what we want if only we will be good, not pout and not cry. We are too often inclined to tell God that we will do what pleases the Almighty, if God will just do what pleases us.

A young man at the university where I teach was trying to date a coed on campus. She did not seem particularly interested in him, so he came to my office to talk about what he should do that would get her to turn on to him. He suggested that prayer might be just the thing, and wondered if that would be an okay thing to do. "After all," he said, "through prayer all things are possible." He wanted me to join him in his efforts because in the Epistle of James he had read, "the prayers of a righteous man are powerful and effective" (5:6).

I was flattered to think that he considered me a righteous man, but I could not go along with his absurd scheme. I asked him instead whether he was surrendered to the will of God, whatever it might be, or if he was trying to pressure God to fulfill his own personal wishes.

This young man believed in a God who could be manipulated for his purposes and who would manipulate others on his behalf, if only the right prayer formula was used. I had a hard time convincing him to the contrary.

As of late, I have seen a very interesting attempt to manipulate God, called "tithing your way to riches." Some preach that one-tenth of the money *you would like to make* should be given over to "the work of God" (specifically, to the work of God done by that preacher's ministry). If you give a tithe on the money you hope to have, the idea goes, then God will give you nine times your tithe in the future—that is, the income you want. Some hopeful people have taken all of the money at their disposal and handed it over to a preacher who promised that God would provide a tenfold return on that investment. Such giving, claimed the preacher, puts God into a state of obligation in which God would have to deliver.

I need not critique such claims for you to see how wrongheaded that is. What upsets me most is that this teaching has become common in many developing countries. The poorest of the poor are being ripped off while the preachers who collect from them live in luxury.

WHAT PRAYER DOES

I do not want to leave the impression that prayer does not accomplish anything or that it is without effect. I earnestly believe that intercessory prayer can surround the prayed-for person with the love of God in a special way. Prayer can reap wonderful spiritual blessings. Through prayer, we become surrendered instruments through whom God's love can move.

We tend to think of prayer as the means of getting God to reach out to touch or even transform another person. God is able to do that directly, but I'd like to suggest that prayer is also the means by which God can flow through us to reach that other person. Through prayer we become "sending agents" of God's love; channels through whom the passionate love of God flows out to and engulfs other people. The more faithful Christians we get to join us as channels through whom the infinite love of God can flow, the more likely it will be that the Spirit will invade the person for whom we pray and do what human persuasion alone could never do.

Consider how Jesus prayed. He was not out to change His Father's will, but rather to become a surrendered instrument through whom the Father could do great and wonderful things. Jesus said, "Not as I will, but as you will" (Matt. 26:39). He was not trying to change God's mind, but rather was offering Himself up to His Father as an instrument through whom the heavenly Father could express love that would change the world. Jesus was constantly praying and fasting in order to be God's perfect instrument. If we, through prayer and fasting, would become imitators of Jesus' prayer style, God would use us as well.

Prayer does not produce magical results. God flowing through us to a particular person may enable that person to sense the glory of God in very significant and enticing ways, but even with all that praying, that person can still say no to what God wants to do in his or her life. That is why there is a hell, and that is why people go there. People who refuse to yield to the love of God, who stubbornly resist the Holy Spirit, create their own painful consequences. People can willfully reject God, turning their backs on God's love and rendering the prayers of the faithful ineffective.

I always remind those who pray earnestly for their friends and family members that Jesus Himself had family members who rejected Him. He had several brothers, but only a few came to acknowledge Him as Lord. The others, like many for whom we pray, rejected His pleading love. If Jesus refused to override the rebellious wills of some of His own brothers, than we must not assume that it will be otherwise with our relatives and friends. We must pray for them because it is through prayer that the loving presence of Christ can impact their lives and become dramatically real to them, but we cannot guarantee the salvation of loved ones through prayer. Prayer is not a manipulative, magical power. It is simply the love of God flowing through us to them.

I am fully aware of the implications of what I am suggesting, but I am convinced that those implications are in accord with the teachings of Scripture. If what I have said about prayer is valid and biblically sound, then we are participants with God in reaching the lost with the love of God. This, I believe, is what the Bible is saying when it states that we are "fellow laborers" together with God for the salvation of the lost (see 2 Cor. 6:1).

God invites us to be part of His plan for reaching the lost of the world. Isn't that remarkable? God wants us to be vessels through whom His transforming presence is experienced by those who are thirsty for life. No other honor can accord us more dignity and importance than God's faith in us to be instruments of the Spirit's love!

What I have said implies that God can do through us what God did through Christ Jesus. But this is exactly what Jesus taught when He said:

> I tell you the truth, anyone who has faith in me will do what I have been doing. He will do even greater things than these, because I am going to the Father (John 14:12).

The time has come for us to turn away from forms of religiosity that Malinowski properly called magic. Prayer must not be reduced to playing power games with God. True religion should never attempt to manipulate God. Instead, we must surrender to God's will and to God's service. In true religion, God is able to use us to bless others, as James wrote in his epistle:

Religion that God our Father accepts as pure and faultless is this: to look after orphans and widows in their distress and to keep oneself from being polluted by the world (Jas. 1:27).

Prayerful people who become channels for God's love are always a blessing to others.

HOLY TERRORS

Few people know the rhetoric of servanthood better than the clergy, yet so many of them, perhaps unconsciously, are on power trips. Some were likely attracted to the preaching ministry because they saw in it an opportunity to exercise power. Clergypersons of this type learn to play their power games with a cleverness that keeps most people from suspecting what they are really all about.

One of the clever ways a minister tries to gain and maintain power is to do all the work of the church. This "servanthood" makes it difficult for other church members to challenge what the pastor wants to do. On the surface it all looks like loving service, but it is a power play.

As a young pastor, I was guilty of this tactic. I relieved the deacons of any responsibility for visiting sick or shut-in church members, and did it all myself. I ran the youth groups and the Vacation Bible School. I supervised the Sunday School, mimeographed the church bulletin, organized the church choir, unofficially chaired every committee and did half of the janitorial work. For the most part, the church people stood back in amazement at my boundless energy and seeming dedication, largely unaware that, by doing all that I did, I was keeping church members out of positions of leadership. I was in charge of everything. I controlled the church and my power was evident everywhere.

When church members wanted to take over some of the roles I had monopolized, I felt threatened by them. When there were meetings with fellow clergy in my community, our discussion often evolved around how to handle such uppity members. I would ask questions such as "Don't they realize what I am trying to accomplish?" and "Why do they want to hold me back?" and "Why are they interfering with my plans?" and "Don't they understand that if they would just move out of my way, I could really get this church rolling?"

I am sure these thoughts and actions are common to many young pastors just out of seminary, and I wonder how many give up on being pastors simply because they cannot have their own way or persuade their church members to comply with their every dictate. I also wonder how many church members have been stymied in their spiritual growth because they have not had opportunities to exercise their gifts within the Body of Christ. Scripture teaches that God gives gifts to *all* Christians and that each should be allowed to exercise his or her gift. Unfortunately, some clergypersons act as if the ordained minister is the entire Body of Christ and is responsible for everything. This leaves little room for anyone else to do anything significant within the life of the church.

Ideally, a minister should recognize that his or her obligation is to enable other church members to take over the various responsibilities essential to the ministry of a healthy congregation. As a good leader, the pastor should help members discover their respective gifts and abilities and how these talents can be used in the work of the church. The pastor should train members to effectively exercise their gifts to meet the needs of the rest of the congregation and to minister to the world outside the church. This is what Paul was suggesting in his letter to the Ephesians:

It was [Christ] who gave some to be apostles, some to be prophets, some to be evangelists, and some to be pastors and teachers, to prepare God's people for works of service, so that the body of Christ may be built up (Eph. 4:11-12).

80

Pastors who try to do everything themselves often complain about the lack of adequate lay leadership in their churches, but in reality, they are keeping lay workers out of leadership roles because of their own need for power. Sometimes a power-hungry pastor cons his congregation into hiring an assistant pastor who can, in turn, be controlled. Then the two of them are able to do all the church work and it becomes unnecessary for church members to do anything at all. The pastor, in such a case, becomes more powerful than ever. The church programs grind on, while the laity remains unchallenged and dormant and the church dies spiritually.

I presently belong to a church of almost 3,000 members. Our pastor has a brilliant capacity to move members of the church to do many tasks that are often considered the prerogative of professional clergy. The result is a dynamic congregation with responsible leadership and only one paid assistant. My pastor finds it unnecessary to play power games. He loves his people and they love him. Love is always a possibility when power is set aside.

THE POWERLESS BUT LOVING PROPHET

Prophets are seldom people of power. It is all but impossible to simultaneously be prophetic and hold a position of power. While being prophetic is the responsibility of every minister, declaring the hard judgments of God can have an adverse effect on the preacher's ability to lead. It is not surprising, therefore, that there are many ministers who are afraid to declare what the Bible says about the prominent evils at work in our society and in our churches because their church members might become angry and alienated. The prophet comes with a word of judgment on existing social conditions and on the behavior of the people, but also must recognize that he or she is not separated from the people, as though he or she is not guilty of the same sins. The prophetic preacher declares the word of the Lord for the people and for himself or herself.

The *prophet* is called to be a disturber of those who have become comfortable in a lukewarm commitment to Christ. The *pastor*, on the other hand, is called to comfort people and to nurture them. Whereas the prophet is a divisive voice, the pastor is supposed to be an agent of reconciliation. When Jesus exercised His prophetic calling, He said, "Do not suppose that I have come to bring peace to the earth. I did not come to bring peace, but a sword" (Matt. 10:34), and it's no wonder they crucified Him. The pastor knows that being prophetic could get him or her crucified, too. Yet comforting the troubled and troubling the comfortable are required of anyone who occupies the pulpit.

In ancient biblical history, this conflict did not exist, because these two roles were differentiated. The priest in the Temple performed the pastoral roles of nurturing people and serving as counselors for reconciliation; the prophets were special persons who came into the city from the outside and shouted at the people, "Thus sayeth the Lord!" It is very difficult to play these two conflicting roles simultaneously as the leader of a local church congregation.

When I speak at ministerial conferences and at seminaries, I am usually asked to address social issues. Consequently, I talk about what the Bible says about racism, the poor, war, peace, capital punishment, homophobia and other controversial subjects. Inevitably, some preacher will come up to me afterward and say, "If I verbalized some of the things you said today, I would be without a pulpit."

I usually answer, "I know!"

What the pastor recognizes is that I can speak as I do because there is no way my audience can get back at me. Other than choosing not to invite me back (which is sometimes the case), those to whom I speak cannot take anything away from me. I am not dependent on them, so they cannot strip me of my symbols of office. Because I have nothing to lose, I am free to say what I believe the Scripture teaches and let the chips fall where they may. I am not a leader of a congregation, and this powerlessness frees me to be prophetic. My age also has something to do with it. As of this writing, I am 74 years old, and I am no longer out to make a name for myself or to become important. Giving up the seeking of prestige, which is a form of power, is a very freeing thing for anyone who wants to do the work of a prophet.

I want to emphasize that being the pastor of a local church does not preclude the possibility of being prophetic or preaching on controversial issues, but I think we must acknowledge that combining these two roles is difficult. If a pastor is going to be prophetic—and to be faithful to God, the pastor must do this—then that pastor should do so in a spirit of love, praying that love will enable the people to hear what must be said. I also want to emphasize that loving sacrifice can earn authority that will invite the congregation to listen to hard messages.

I once heard a story about William Sloan Coffin. This one-time preacher of the great Riverside Church in New York City preached several sermons during the years of the Vietnam War that condemned America's participation in that conflict. After one of those sermons, a member of the congregation, an officer in the military, marched up to him and angrily blurted, "It was all I could do to keep my seat when you preached that message. I wanted to stand up, stomp out the center aisle and yell back at you, 'Bull***!'"

Reverend Coffin asked, "Why didn't you?"

This high-ranking officer said meekly, "Because the night my wife died, you stayed up all night, sitting at her bedside, holding her hand and praying with her."

The loving service of a pastor can create the *authority* necessary to be a prophetic voice.

SPEAKING THE TRUTH IN LOVE

Too often a congregation is turned off not so much by what a pastor says, but by the manner in which it is said. When a pastor speaks like a demagogue or proclaims a message with arrogance, a strong negative reaction will almost always be elicited from the listeners. If a preacher acts as if hers is the final interpretation of Scripture or is the only viable way of understanding the Bible, hearers will turn away. On the other hand, should the preacher approach the congregation in love, conveying that the message about current social issues is being offered with fear and trembling, and emphasizing the possibility that he or she could be wrong, the congregation may be willing to hear out the message with their hearts as well as their ears.

Any controversial prophetic message should be coupled with an invitation to discuss what had been said, with a focus on whether or not the message had been faithful to the words of Scripture. The prophetic preacher must be able to make the case that the Bible supports what was declared from the pulpit. Yet even in such a discussion, there should be an acknowledgement from the preacher that his or her word is not infallible. The members of the congregation should view the preacher as one who, along with them, is faithfully struggling to understand the whole counsel of God. They should feel invited to join the preacher in the struggle for truth, so that together they might begin to grasp how God wants them to respond to the controversial matter at hand. It's a good idea to meet with those with contrary opinions. A meeting following the service or scheduled for a not-too-distant future time is a pastoral response to a difficult and disturbing prophetic message. When the preacher does not confront the congregation from a position of power, it is amazing how open the members can be. When they sense that the message comes from someone who loves them, rather than from someone who condemns or despises them for their "limited vision," they are more likely to grant to the preacher a high level of openness. If I could write a Beatitude for preachers, it would be:

> Blessed are you when people reject you because you declared the judgment of God with loving conviction and with tears in your eyes; but cursed are you if they reject God's word because of the way in which you declared it and the attitudes that they discerned in you.

Pastors must learn that they cannot impose their views on their congregations as though they are especially ordained to be mouthpieces for God. To demand compliance with personal views is arrogant. Only Christ Himself has the right to speak above contradiction or correction. This is not to suggest that there is no room for stern and bold proclamation, but any declaration that begins with, "Thus sayeth the Lord!" should be delivered only after much prayer and fasting. Even then, it should be uttered with fear and trembling, and should come only after every possible approach in love has been made.

One more thing should be added to these proposals: A good prophet must go beyond a call to repentance. To be truly prophetic, the message must also provide for the people a clear alternative for the future. For instance, to simply tell people that they are living lives of affluence in the midst of a world of poverty is to create guilt and guilt alone. But if, added to such a declaration, the people are also told specific things they can do to respond in love to the needs of the poor and to alleviate the sufferings of the oppressed, they likely will do so. They need to see exactly what they can do to change who they are and to address the social evils they have been made to confront. The true prophet should be ready to join the people, so that together they can seek new ways of living in a world that not only needs prophetic preaching, but also requires prophetic action.

LONE RANGERS FOR JESUS

The destructiveness of pastoral power was horribly exemplified years ago in the saga of Jim Jones and The Peoples Temple. The world was shocked when, under his influence and command, nearly a thousand of his followers committed suicide in the jungles of Guyana. Yet those who have traced the history and development of his leadership and the movement that he generated have positive things to say about the early ministry of Jim Jones. His early theology and behavior, though somewhat unorthodox, could hardly be considered socially deviant. His preaching was helpful to many troubled people. Some testified that through Jones's ministry and his church, The Peoples Temple, they had been rescued from lifestyles that otherwise would have spelled their doom. Drug addicts were delivered from dependency on heroin; alcoholics found release from their sickness; prostitutes recovered a sense of dignity and started life anew. The stories of people helped by Jim Jones go on and on. Through The Peoples Temple, he had an extensive social ministry, providing assistance for poor people, exercising a positive influence on the political system of Los Angeles and even encouraging economic development in a Third World country, Guyana.

However, with Jones's growing successes came growing power. As his movement grew, people gave him more and more adoration for his accomplishments. As his power expanded, Jones gained more control over his followers.

At first, Jones's followers willingly complied with his orders. In time, however, they found that they had almost no other choice. Those who opposed him discovered that he could have them punished and, if need be, even murdered. Love turned into fear as Jones changed from a loving pastor into a powerful demagogue.

That is what happens when a leader's power goes unchecked, and when that leader is responsible to no one else. With unchecked power, leaders often develop messianic complexes and suffer from megaloma-nia. While no pastor in a normal church situation is likely to imitate Jim Jones, many do find themselves transformed by their own sense of power. In too many cases, there are pastors, preachers and evangelists who operate beyond the control of any committee or board of elders or deacons. When this happens, their growing power gradually erodes their spiritual stature and hurts the very people they are supposed to help.

There is little question in my mind but that the televangelist Jim Bakker, who reached the height of his power in the 1980s, is another Christian leader who began as an upright person in the early stages of his ministry, trying to do good things for God and His kingdom. But because there was no one to check his tendencies toward exercising power, he ended up doing things contrary to everything he believed. Jim Bakker was eventually humbled when he was exposed for scandalous behavior and sent to prison. Today, he is a much humbler man and in ministry once more, and we all pray that he doesn't once again fall into the same power pitfalls that previously brought him down.

The ancient Greek philosopher Plato once asked how many people would remain honest if they knew they could transcend the control of others and never be held accountable. We all have diabolical tendencies and destructive desires, but fortunately most of us do not have the power to express them; society prevents us from carrying out the impulses that lie beneath our outward appearances of morality and propriety. According to Plato, if societal restraints were removed, it would not be long before we would evidence cruelties and lustful cravings that would render us extremely dangerous.

The *Lord of the Flies* is a fictional description of what happens when a group of choirboys gets marooned on an island in the middle of the Pacific.[1] Delivered from the restraints of society, they strip away the thin veneer of socially prescribed morality and become power-hungry tyrants.

The novel is a parable of what results when human nature goes unchecked by systems of accountability. Not just such boys, but also all of us—and especially pastors—need external checks on our inward lust for power.

I know of one prominent minister who was a dynamic preacher and a creative leader. His church grew by leaps and bounds until it was one of the largest and most influential in the city of Philadelphia. Because of his charisma, his congregation was in awe of him and never dared to oppose him. His lay leaders were not strong enough to stand up to him, even when they knew he was wrong. His unchecked power, little by little, brought about his downfall. He began to act as though the rules and regulations that he taught for others did not apply to him. He became involved in an extramarital sexual affair that eventually led to his divorce. When his behavior became so outlandish that his congregation finally rose up and wrested his pulpit and power away from him, he acted surprised. He had become so deluded by power that he thought he could do anything and never suffer negative consequences from his actions.

I believe that every pastor should have a select group of people to whom he or she is willing to be submissive and responsible. That group should constantly evaluate the lifestyle of the pastor and call for repentance when needed. In such a situation, the pastor should be yielded to the counsel of the group and be willing to go along with their directives. It is my strong suggestion that this group *not* be composed of members of the pastor's congregation, but should be made up of people from outside the church fellowship who are nonetheless committed, mature Christians.

Whenever an individual Christian functions as a "Lone Ranger for Jesus," that person becomes dangerous to both himself and others. This is why the apostle James instructed that every Christian ought to be in fellowship with a group of fellow believers to whom sins could be confessed and who could provide discipline when needed (see Jas. 5:16).

Without restraints from fellow Christians, each and every one of us is in danger of venting our worst tendencies, with devastating results.

As I reflect on my years as a pastor, I recall the pain and suffering I endured. Some of the struggles and conflicts within the churches where I served made my life miserable. Yet when I reevaluate those difficulties, I see how many of them were the result of my own power plays. In my youthful immaturity, I wanted my own way and had little patience with people who did not go along with me. Many of my plans were good and probably would have increased the outreach of those churches and resulted in congregational growth. However, in trying to force my will on others, my efforts became counter-productive. By trying to operate from a position of power, I alienated the very people I was trying to serve. And when they reacted negatively to my best plans and most creative visions, I was reduced to a bitter, frustrated person who hated being a minister.

POWERFUL MISSIONARIES

Power problems can also sometimes be found among missionaries. Missionary service becomes a means of achieving power if it creates unhealthy dependencies among indigenous people, diminishing the dignity of the very people whom missionaries are endeavoring to serve. If things are done for indigenous people that they can do for themselves, the people become subservient to missionaries who came to serve them. Some missionaries have become deliberately paternalistic, maneuvering themselves into positions of power over the very people they claim to be reaching with the gospel. By choosing to do more than they should, they either consciously or unconsciously gain power over the people. There have been too many cases of missionaries buying the allegiance of indigenous people through the provision of schools, medical care and economic opportunities. Paternalism in missionary work is a power play that must be resisted. When missionaries are paternalistic, indigenous people are made to feel that they owe something to the missionaries and are cowed into obedience. It is no wonder that such people often turn away from Christianity when the social and economic benefits derived from such submission are no longer forthcoming.

While in Haiti, I remember meeting with a medical missionary who had spent his life sacrificially giving of himself to people in that impoverished country. In return, however, he expected that the Haitians he served should be in awe of him. It was painful for him to realize as he came to the end of his life that the people he had sought to serve failed to become the mature Christians he had hoped they would be—nor did he feel they appreciated all he had done for them. Because he hadn't thought them capable of exercising roles of leadership and had held all the power himself, he had kept them from developing into the kind of people God wanted them to be. Paternalistic missionaries can stymie effective discipleship and church growth.

Even more pathetic are missionaries who have learned to enjoy positions of power on the mission field, only to return home expecting to live normal lives. Often, they cannot make the adjustment. They cannot tolerate being ordinary church members within a local congregation, no longer enjoying the power and prestige they experienced on the field. They may long to return to the place where they were the powerful ones, in charge of everything. Sometimes they are critical of their pastors, demonstrate superiority over other church members and become such malcontents that the rest of the church would be happy if they were to leave.

In the late 1940s when Communists took over in China, the work of Western missionaries was suppressed. Almost all were sent home to their nations of origin, and many Western Christians assumed that Christianity would die in China. As mission schools and hospitals were nationalized, some predicted the complete annihilation of more than a century of missionary work. But just the opposite happened. The church in China grew from about 900,000 to more than 70 million today.[2] When the powerful presence of missionaries was removed, the Chinese church blossomed as never before.

In Africa, the same sort of thing happened. As missionaries withdrew, the church grew—from 10 million Christians south of the Sahara in 1965 to more than 100 million today.[3] Almost 23,000 new members are added to African churches every single day through the efforts of indigenous pastors, rather than through the efforts of powerful outside missionaries and the agencies they represent.[4]

Of course, there are instances of indigenous pastors going on power trips, and there are legitimate fears for the future of locally grown Christianity under such leaders. All Christian servants, regardless of their country of origin or their mission field—local or foreign—must be on guard against what power can do when they forget that they are called to be servants.

Jesus reserved some of His harshest words for the religious leaders of His day who lorded their power over others. Jesus said, "Woe to you Pharisees, because you love the most important seats in the synagogues and greetings in the marketplaces" (Luke 11:43). Their delight in their own power would be their undoing, and He warned His disciples against falling prey to the same temptation. He said, "whoever wants to become great among you must be your servant" (Matt. 20:26). That command stands for anyone who answers His call today.

GLORIOUS AUTHORITY

During the first century of its existence, the Church was a powerless movement. Its members were, for the most part, working-class people and slaves. The apostle Paul wrote about the composition of the Early Church in 1 Corinthians 1:26-29:

> Brothers [and sisters], think of what you were when you were called. Not many of you were wise by human standards; not many were influential; not many were of noble birth. But God chose the foolish things of the world to shame the wise; God chose the weak things of the world to shame the strong. He chose the lowly things of this world and the despised things—and the things that are not—to nullify the things that are, so that no one may boast before him.

These early followers of Jesus could hardly be called the movers and shakers of the Roman world; nevertheless, they made a decisive difference throughout the Roman Empire. They won converts in great numbers. They sent missionaries to carry the gospel into Europe, Africa and Asia. They challenged the morality of the existing social structure. Though the Church commanded no armies and held no political power, it threatened the lifestyle of the Roman Empire enough to warrant the wrath of its emperors. Historians generally agree that the Church was, in those days, doing great things—and they did it without power.

In 313 A.D., the Christian Church went through a major transition that changed its character. In that year, the Emperor Constantine gave official recognition to Christianity and provided it with a favored status; Christianity became the unofficial religion of the Roman Empire. Seemingly overnight, people throughout the Roman domain had to adjust to having a "born-again" emperor. From this dubious honor, the Church has not recovered. Under the favor of Constantine, the Church moved from being a despised, persecuted and intensely spiritually dedicated minority to being a guise for continued imperial conquest. The Church moved into dominance throughout the Roman Empire. Its leaders were no longer renegades and outlaws, but persons who wielded substantial political power. The general consensus of Church historians is that the moment Christianity allied itself with the power of the state, it entered into a period of corruption and disintegration, gradually losing much of its moral authority and spiritual dynamism.

I believe that the Church was not meant to wield power and that when it did, it betrayed its calling as the primary agent of God's love. As the Church increased in power, it decreased in authority. It came to be known more by the power its bishops wielded than the sacrifices made by its people.

After Constantine, the Church changed from a persecuted body of believers into a persecuting institution, often putting to death those who deviated from its doctrine. The Church was gradually transformed from a community that sent out missionaries to win the world to Christ into a crusading army that would, centuries later, march on the Arab world to bring death and suffering to millions. The Church failed to understand that political power, especially in the hands of those who are religious, annihilates love. Love, in its sacrificial form, is what the pure Church is supposed to be all about, and when it resorts to power to promote its agenda, it forfeits its calling.

SEEKING POWER: THE RELIGIOUS LEFT AND THE RELIGIOUS RIGHT

Unfortunately, the Church has not learned from the tragedies of history and has frequently repeated its mistakes. During the 1950s and 1960s, the leaders of mainline denominations in the U.S. yielded to the temptation to power. They went knocking on the doors of the White House. Claiming the ability to mobilize the voting power of their members, they demanded that their agenda for social justice be implemented by the state. Today, few would argue against the justice of their cause, but many who espouse progressive political views have come to have regrets about their methods.

The biggest reaction to the Christian Left crystallized by the 1980s: Politically conservative Christians formed what has come to be known as the Religious Right. Learning from those on the Left, they too began to frequent the halls of government in Washington and demand that their agenda be turned into political policy. The Religious Right, following such leaders as Ralph Reed, Jerry Falwell and Pat Robertson, developed an extensive grassroots organization that not only got the attention of leaders on the national level, but also heavily influenced campaigns and policy on the state and local levels. When those on the Left objected to the way the Religious Right was using churches for political purposes, they were reminded that the Religious Left had done the same thing only a few years earlier.

The Religious Right now has at its disposal more than 2,000 "Christian" radio broadcasting organizations.[1] The majority of these stations broadcast not just the gospel, but also the agenda of conservative politics, sometimes deeming those who do not agree with their political ideology to be less than true Christians. Through this effective means of communication (some of the content could justly be called "propaganda"), they have elected candidates who conform to their beliefs and have nurtured, by most accounts, the most powerful lobbying coalition on the contemporary American scene.

Both those on the Religious Left and on the Religious Right believed that if they could just get "their people" into positions of power, they could impose their respective agendas on the rest of the American populace. They thought that the kingdom of God could be made a political reality through the exercise of law and the coercion of the state. In chapter 1, I told you my response: "I wonder why didn't Jesus think of that?" Why didn't Jesus think of coming as a Caesar, with armies to enforce His will? Why did He come as a helpless baby in the manger and grow up to be the suffering Servant?

The answer to such questions is that He came to bring the world to God through sacrificial love.

One of my friends, an ardent member of the Moral Majority, points out that all he is trying to do is employ the same methods Christian liberals used during the 1960s, when they worked for an end to the war in Vietnam and to racial segregation. My friend claims that mainline Christians never questioned using political power to pursue Christian causes until they realized that conservative Christians could also play power games. In short, he finds it hypocritical for liberals to push their social programs through the use of political power and then criticize conservatives when they adopt the same techniques.

My friend is right in his criticism. While I am a conservative Christian in matters of theology, I hold many political views that my critics consider liberal. My Religious Right friend correctly notes that I had nothing to say when the leaders of the National Council of Churches used any and all political pressure tactics available to end apartheid in South Africa and to work for women's rights; therefore, he says, it is hypocritical for me to get upset today when the Religious Right exercises its considerable political power. All I can say to his criticism is that I did not give much thought to a biblical perspective on power until the Religious Right used it effectively. We often do not see the wrong in our own behavior until we see the same behavior from those who disagree with us.

I am not debating the rightness or wrongness of the political positions taken by the Religious Right or the Religious Left, nor am I condemning their desire to create a better America. The Religious Right puts a strong emphasis on family life, and improvements in this area are desperately needed. Its condemnation of the decline of ethical standards that have made our society decent is very timely. Their indignation over the relentless imposition of secular humanist values on the American consciousness is much needed. The Religious Left also has a commendable agenda: to end racism, sexism, militarism, poverty and homophobia. Rather than their particular agendas, what concerns me are the *methods* employed to bring about the changes each of these groups desires. Both sides are too easily tempted to use and depend on the power of the state to enforce their will on the rest of the populace. This is a serious mistake that will, in the long run, hurt the witness of the Church and significantly diminish its authority. Only when the Church speaks with the authority it earns through its people living out sacrificial love will it again become the revolutionary movement that can change in the world—the movement it is called to be.

A good example of how the Church trades power for authority and tarnishes its witness can be seen in the passing of Proposition 8 in California in 2008. Evangelical Christians, joining together with the Roman Catholic Church and the Mormons, led an effort to put an end to gay marriages, which California courts had earlier declared legal. They organized to pass a change in the state's constitution to assure that marriage could be only between one man and one woman, thus overturning the courts' ruling. These powerful religious allies brought an army of canvassers into the state and spent nearly $40 million to advertise what they believed were the dangers to traditional family life if gay marriage was not put to an end.[2]

The day after polls closed, the leaders of this anti-gay-marriage movement declared victory. But even as they basked in the aura of their success, I asked myself, *What did they win?*

Did Harry and John end their homosexual liaison because Proposition 8 had passed?

Did Mary and Jane not climb into bed together that night because the power of the Church had been used to make such marriages null and void?

Of course not! Nothing had changed except this: Tens of thousands of gays and lesbians marched on the streets of San Francisco, Los Angeles, New York, Chicago and scores of other cities in protest, many cursing the Church. From their point of view, Jesus was their enemy and the Bible was a handbook for their oppression! If you call this winning, then you and I have very different definitions of the word.

The Church flexed its political muscles, and in doing so it lost a good bit of its authority. It's not likely that the gay community saw much of the love of God through the Church's actions, and I predict that it will be a long time before they consider us Christians anything like the "instruments of God's love" we are called to be.

I am *not* suggesting, for one moment, that the people of God should refrain from changing the world—quite the opposite. But God wants to transform the world through followers of Jesus who are yielded and open to what the Spirit wants to do in them, not by employing coercive power as a means to bring about justice. Jesus warned the disciples against using worldly coercion in Matthew 20:25-26: "You know that the rulers of the Gentiles lord it over them, and their high officials exercise authority over them. Not so with you. Instead, whoever wants to become great among you must be your servant."

I am absolutely convinced that Jesus saves us from sin primarily to make us into world-changers. Getting into heaven when we die is very much a part of the gospel, but Jesus had much more to say about *how* we should function in this world as agents of change. Reading through the New Testament, it's obvious that Jesus did not die on the cross *only* to save us from hell and get us into heaven (though His death on the cross makes both of these things possible). Jesus also died to make us into a holy people, through whom He could change this world into what He created it to be. We are saved, says the eighth chapter of Romans, to respond to the cries for deliverance that we hear coming to us from all corners of God's creation (see Rom. 8:18-22). Through those who are yielded to His will, God wants to invade all parts of the social order and transform the world into the kingdom of God. Jesus came declaring that kingdom; He announced it in the first words out of His mouth, as recorded in the Gospels of Matthew, Mark and Luke. When we pray the Lord's Prayer, we pray, "Thy Kingdom come, Thy will be done on earth as it is in Heaven." Through those who are possessed by the Holy Spirit, He seeks to challenge the "rulers and authorities in the heavenly realms"—principalities and the realms they influence, governments, economic structures, the media, educational institutions—to bring them under His domain (see Eph. 3:10).

But each in his own turn: Christ, the firstfruits; then, when he comes, those who belong to him. Then the end will come, when he hands over the kingdom to God the Father after he has destroyed all dominion, authority and power. For he must reign until he has put all his enemies under his feet (1 Cor. 15:23-25).

At the end of the first chapter of Ephesians, the apostle Paul makes clear that our Lord wants to bring all principalities and all social institutions into subjection to the will of God—*through the Church*:

He raised [Christ] from the dead and seated him at his right hand in the heavenly realms, far above all rule and authority, power and dominion, and every title that can be given, not only in the present age but also in the one to come. And God placed all things under his feet and appointed him to be head over everything for the church, which is his body, the fullness of him who fills everything in every way (Eph. 1:20-23).

Christians are motivated by a divine imperative to be agents of transformation, instruments of social change and participants in God's revolution. This is not a reworked version of the old social gospel, wherein some liberal Christians imagined that we, through our activism, could change this messed up world into the kingdom of God. No, this is a call to participate *with* God in the work God is doing in this world, realizing that His kingdom will only come in fullness with the second coming of Christ. God is at work *right now*, transforming the world through those who are yielded and open to what the Spirit wants to do in them and through them, in preparation for the day He returns in glory to complete the good work He has already begun (see Phil. 1:6).

For me, there is no question that we are to be involved with what happens in the world. We are to be the salt of the earth that permeates all areas of life with the love of God (see Matt. 5:13). We are to effect change in society just as leaven changes dough in the process of making bread (see Matt. 13:33).

We must always remember the words of Martin Luther King, Jr., who once said, "The church must be reminded that it is not the master or the servant of the state, but rather the conscience of the state."[3] In the U.S., we have the doctrine of separation of church and state for good reason. We don't want the government controlling the Church;

neither do we want the Church controlling the government. Given Dr. King's insight, how then are we to live out our responsibility to do God's work in the world?

By what means should we seek to alter society? In what ways should we give expression to the love of God in the social institutions of our modern world? Before we go any further, we ought to remember the words of Zechariah, who declared that the rebuilding of the Temple would be done " 'not by might nor by power, but by my Spirit,' says the LORD Almighty" (Zech. 4:6).

GOD'S METHODS
FOR SOCIAL CHANGE

A few years ago, some of my Eastern University students did a study of the social structures and systems of the Dominican Republic. They chose to study that little nation because the missionary organization that I had helped to establish (the Evangelical Association for the Promotion of Education) had been developing a variety of educational programs there. As our students researched, they became disturbed when they found out that the nation was dominated by a multi-national corporation that produced sugar. This company, Gulf & Western, pretty much controlled the eastern half of the nation. Not only was Gulf & Western into sugar, it also had a major stake in hotels, golf courses and other facilities that catered to the growing tourist industry. The company was so entrenched in the Dominican Republic that any initiative to bring greater justice to the Dominican people had to be in cooperation with the movers and shakers within the company. The Marxists of the country talked about overthrowing the government and gaining control of Gulf & Western's assets, then restructuring it "for the good of the people." But our students knew that violence is not the way that Christians should try to accomplish their goals.

Our students decided to buy stock in Gulf & Western. This enabled them to attend stockholders' meetings, where they could champion the changes they thought were essential to the health and wellbeing of the Dominican people. For instance, they believed that any land that could be used to grow food for the indigenous people should be used for that purpose rather than for growing sugar. They also believed that the company should abandon its control of the eastern part of the nation. Furthermore, they wanted to get Gulf & Western to use its vast resources to help diversify the Dominican economy, develop medical and educational programs, and do a variety of other things that would improve the people's quality of life.

Our students joined forces with others with similar concerns, notably the Adrian Dominican Sisters based in the state of Michigan. At first, the students and their allies thought they should seek proxy votes from other stockholders so that they could represent a powerful bloc at the next meeting. They believed they could force the company into accepting their demands.

Fortunately, their efforts to consolidate power failed, and failure drove my students to re-evaluate their methods. They began to reflect on whether or not Jesus would try to force Gulf & Western to do what He knew was right. They asked themselves whether Jesus would employ coercive power as a means to bring about justice.

After much discussion and consideration, they changed their tactics. They asked for a meeting with some of the corporation's executives, aiming to find out firsthand if they would be willing to work along with the students to improve the living conditions of the Dominican people. Much to their surprise (and somewhat to their embarrassment), they found the leaders of Gulf & Western were not at all as the students had imagined. These top executives turned out to be decent people who really wanted to do what was best for the Dominican people—not only because doing so was right, but also because it was good business.

Once the students abandoned their attempt to coerce the company into conforming to their ideas of justice, they found the leaders quite willing to reconsider the corporation's activities in the Dominican Republic. The executives admitted that they were doing things that did not serve the best interests of the Dominican people, and that they were willing to change their practices to whatever degree possible. They demonstrated, in word and in deed, that they wanted to run a fair and equitable business.

One afternoon, I received a telephone call from one of the vice presidents of Gulf & Western. He told me that, the following day, they would be making an announcement to the press that would demonstrate their strong desire to improve the lives of the Dominican people: The company would test all the soil they used to grow sugar, and all the land that was found to be arable for growing food would be utilized for that purpose—instead of for growing sugar. Only land that could not be used to grow food for indigenous consumption would be utilized for sugar production.

Furthermore, the company would commit an investment of $100 million a year in social, economic and educational projects aimed at improving the quality of life for the Dominican Republic. The company would do this for five years, he said, with a total investment of $500 million.

Gulf & Western was listed by some militant social activists as one of the most immoral corporations in the world. Whether that designation was ever justified, I cannot say. But this I do know: Gulf & Western became a shining example of a corporation that tried to exercise moral responsibility in a developing nation. The company proved to be one of the most constructive forces for social change in that troubled nation, and literally transformed the life and character of the eastern half of the Dominican Republic.

What is important for us to recognize here is that the leaders of Gulf & Western did not respond to force and coercion. They would not be intimidated. But when approached in friendship and appeals to conscience, they were responsive to reasonable requests to effect change in their policies.

There are those who think that without coercive power it is impossible to get anything done in today's world. They are convinced that the powerless cannot expect to make the world better. But such people give very little consideration to the style of Jesus, who had power enough to force all humanity to its knees, destroy all evils of society and make all things right. Yet He chose not to save the world through the exercise of power, but rather to change it through His sacrificial love. Christ emptied Himself of all the power and glory of God, and took upon Himself the weaknesses that we associate with living in the flesh. As an old hymn has it, He "emptied Himself of all but love."[4] He would initiate change in the world, but not through the exercise of power.

The story of Bethlehem is not just a sentimental story to touch our hearts at the Christmas season, though it does that. It describes the extent to which Christ was willing to go to save us from sin and bring salvation to His world. He came in the weakness of flesh, and lived among us as a servant. His was a life of simple obedience to the will of His Father. He was obedient, even to the point of dying on the cross. He confronted the powerful, demonic hosts, not with a blazing display of power, but with sacrificial love expressed in His willing death.

At Calvary, we see what the power of Satan can do. We observe the demonic nature of political and religious power infused by evil. The Roman governor and the Hebrew king, on the one hand, and the priests and scribes of the religious system, on the other, conspired together to destroy the Son of God. But on the cross, all their claims of being agents of goodness were stripped away. The principalities and powers were exposed as the power-hungry agents they really were (see Col. 2:15). The cross showed how the depraved nature of demonic powers can be expressed through the rulers of this age. It also demonstrated the love of God in its most perfect form. On the cross, power was confronted by sacrificial love.

On Good Friday, it looked as though power had won. The demonic hosts must have danced in celebration. But they had counted the spoils of their victory too quickly. Two days later, the stone was rolled away and the incarnation of sacrificial love was resurrected. History, from then on, would have hard evidence that love ultimately triumphs over power. The resurrection proves that love is greater than all the power man and Satan together can muster.

The resurrected Christ still endeavors to effect change through love. He does not coerce us into His kingdom, but lovingly entreats us. He does not force Himself into our lives, but instead says, "Here I am! I stand at the door and knock. If anyone hears my voice and opens the door, I will come in and eat with him, and he with me" (Rev. 3:20).

One of my favorite old gospel songs has as its first line, "He could have called ten thousand angels."[5] This so wonderfully explains the style of Jesus. As He hung on the cross, the Pharisees and priests mocked Him, yelling that if He was the Son of God, He should come down from the cross—and then they would believe in Him (see Matt. 27:40-42). There is no question that He could have done just that. What is more, He could have snapped His fingers and had 10,000 angels in shining raiment appear instantaneously by His side, armed to the teeth, to wreak destruction on those who had mocked Him. But that was not His way. Love kept Him nailed to the cross. He refused to use His power so that He might reveal the love of God in its ultimate expression.

There will come a day when He will come again. On that final day, a trumpet will sound and He will unleash His power on the earth. But on that Good Friday 2,000 years ago, it was not His power, but His sacrificial love that was at work.

JESUS' STYLE: NON-VIOLENCE

Many Christians who would say "Amen" to all of this fail to see how the style of Jesus is the model we should follow today in our mission to change the world. They do not understand that Jesus established a pattern that He expects all His followers to imitate.

Among those in recent times who have dared to imitate the style of Jesus was Martin Luther King, Jr. In his efforts to bring social justice to African-Americans oppressed by limited civil rights, King called for non-violent marches and public demonstrations. On one fateful afternoon, hundreds of King's followers staged a march from Selma, Alabama, toward the capital city of Montgomery to demonstrate their commitment to end racial segregation. On live television, millions of people watched as the marchers tried to cross a bridge just outside of Selma, only to have their way barred by a sheriff and his deputies.

The marchers were told to turn back, but they responded, "We've come too far to turn back now."

The sheriff gave a second warning. But the marchers, instead of turning back, went down on their knees in prayer. After a countdown from 10, the sheriff and his followers charged in among the kneeling demonstrators, bashing their heads with billy clubs and unleashing vicious police dogs to attack them.

America saw it all happen on their television sets. The nation witnessed the brutalizing of people who were asking for nothing more than their inalienable rights as Americans. It was a heartbreaking and shocking sight to behold.

Yet even as I watched the horror unfold, something inside me said, *They've won! The civil rights marchers have just won!*

There were many who looked on that scene who did not see victory. Instead, they saw people beaten down. They thought that there was no way the Civil Rights Movement could ever succeed, given what they had witnessed on that bridge just outside the city of Selma. What they saw was defeat. What they did *not* realize is that those who embrace Christ's call for love and justice and adopt His way of changing the world have a nasty habit of rising again, because there is no power on earth that can keep love down. Love never fails (see 1 Cor. 13:8).

Anyone ignorant of the ways of Christ would not understand how a few hundred civil rights activists, battered with clubs and bitten by dogs, could be called winners. To the uninitiated in the ways of Jesus, the sheriff and his helmeted deputies were the victors. Those who chased the civil rights marchers from the bridge seemed to have the upper hand that day; the blood of those activists, called "uppity blacks" by some, was all over the road. Everyone who had only ever trusted in power asked how anyone could consider this a victory—because they did not understand the style of the One who promised that the meek would inherit the earth (see Matt. 5:5).

Even before the confrontation on the Edmund Pettus Bridge, Lyndon B. Johnson, President of the United States, had wanted to enact civil rights legislation. But he had told Dr. King over and over that America was not yet ready. After the confrontation at Selma, however, the president told King that the nation had been made ready.

Love expressed sacrificially overcomes the agencies of power. And so it was that the Civil Rights Act of 1964 was shortly thereafter signed into law. On the bridge outside of Selma, a victory had been won through weakness; a battle had been won through sacrificial non-violence.

SACRIFICE SPEAKS LOUDER THAN WORDS

Many years ago when I was a student, I, along with some of my friends, went to New York to hear the great Toyohiko Kagawa deliver a sermon at Union

Theological Seminary. During World War II, Kagawa worked ceaselessly and daringly to rescue American pilots shot down during bombing raids over Japanese cities. It broke his heart to see the effects of these bombings on his own people, but his Christian commitment led him to love his enemies and to care for those who were injured, frightened and in need. At peril to himself, he visited American pilots who had been stranded in an alien land, bringing them food and binding up their wounds. In helping these prisoners, he denied himself the food and care necessary to keep himself from getting certain diseases, including tuberculosis.

When Kagawa spoke at Union Seminary that day, his voice was hardly audible, and his words seemed merely to be a simple statement of the gospel—not at all the philosophical defense of pacifism we had perhaps been expecting. As he spoke, a seminarian sitting next to me said to his friend, "He doesn't seem to be saying much, does he?"

An elderly woman sitting in front of me turned and said sharply to the two young men, "A man on a cross doesn't have to say anything at all!"

What an incredible statement.

President Ronald Reagan, at a National Prayer Breakfast in Washington, DC, spoke about a Catholic monk from the city of Arles, France, who wanted to visit the Holy City. According to the president's story, when the monk got to Rome, he was swept up in a crowd heading toward the great Coliseum. He had heard that there were to be all kinds of circus displays in the Coliseum, but he did not know that there would also be gladiator fights that day in which doomed men would be called on to fight each other to the death.

Sitting with thousands of others in the seats of the Coliseum, he watched as the gladiators came out of their prison hole, stood before Caesar, saluted him and said, "We, who are about to die, salute thee!" It was only then that the young monk realized what was going to happen. These men were going to try to kill each other!

He stood and shouted, "In the name of Jesus, stop!"

Needless to say, no one listened. The crowd, yelling and cheering for the fights to commence, drowned out his plea.

Again, the young monk shouted, "In the name of Jesus, stop!" And still no one listened.

In desperation, he rushed down to the barrier that separated the spectators from the floor of the arena, jumped over the barrier and ran, screaming, toward the gladiators. "In the name of Jesus, stop! In the name of Jesus, stop!"

He positioned himself between two of the gladiators and pleaded with each to stop in the name of Christ. Instead of listening, the gladiators ran his body through with their swords. He slumped to the ground, dead.

An eerie silence fell upon the crowd, and an unnatural stillness filled the Coliseum. Then, one man toward the back rows of the stadium got up, left his seat, walked down the long aisle of that vast stadium and left. Another followed suit, then another and another, and another and another. Eventually, Caesar himself got out of his seat and left. Little by little, the Coliseum was emptied.

From that day forward, there was never another gladiator fight in the Roman Empire. The age of the gladiators had come to an end. A social system had been transformed, not through political power, but through an act of sacrificial love.[6]

Two Jesuses

In the ancient Hebraic world, Jesus had what we might call a last name. His full name was Jesus bar-Joseph. The word "bar" roughly can be translated as "son of"; thus Jesus bar-Joseph was Jesus, the son of Joseph.

The name Yeshua (in Hebrew; Jesus is the name rendered in Greek) was a common name in the ancient world, a tribute to Joshua, the patriarch who led the children of Israel into the Promised Land. All over Judea, in Jesus bar-Joseph's time, parents named their sons after Joshua, Israel's original deliverer (for that is what the name means). They did so out of a fervent hope that God would send another deliverer, this time to liberate them from the tyrannous oppression of the Romans. They longed for one to come who would restore the kingdom of Israel to the greatness it had known under David and Solomon.

Other than Jesus bar-Joseph, there was, according to Church tradition, another boy in Nazareth named Yeshua. This other Jesus was the son of a man named Rabbas, making his full name Jesus bar-Abbas. These two young Jesuses may have grown up together, sat under the same teachers in school and gone together to the same synagogue on the Sabbath. Both of them likely had dreams, as did other Jewish youth, of restoring the throne of David to Mount Zion and seeing the reign of YHWH come to earth.

There was a difference between them, however: the way each envisioned the kingdom becoming a reality.

Jesus bar-Abbas apparently believed that the only way it could be done was through military conquest. *After all*, thought Jesus bar-Abbas, *that's how Joshua had established the kingdom centuries earlier, and there's no doubt David was a warrior-king.* It was by the sword, he thought, that the kingdom of God would be created. Jesus bar-Abbas was sure of that.

The other Jesus gradually came to the awareness that it could not be by might or power that the kingdom would come but by, as the prophet Zechariah had said, the spiritual leadership of the King of kings and the Lord of lords (see Zech. 4:6).

It may be that each of these boys grew into manhood demonstrating leadership ability and charismatic gifts. But as they reached adulthood, they went their separate ways. Jesus bar-Abbas took up with a group of zealots who came to be known as the Sicarii. They were a group of radical insurgents, who derived their name from the long, curved knives they carried and who lived in the Judean hills. They would sneak out of their caves to raid those they deemed traitors to Israel and used their deadly knives on Romans—and anyone who cooperated with them. They were particularly notorious for wandering into crowded marketplaces and, hidden within the pushing and shoving of the crowd, slipping their knives into "collaborators." With a swift turn of the blade, they could cut out the innards of such traitors to the Hebrew homeland. To the Romans the Sicarii were terrorists, but to many of the Jews, looking for deliverance from the oppressing Roman armies, they were viewed as heroes.

While Jesus bar-Abbas and his followers lived in the hillside caves and staged their guerrilla attacks on both Roman soldiers and those who partnered with them, Jesus bar-Joseph stayed in Nazareth, taking care of His family. We're not sure about the details, but it is probable that Joseph died while Jesus was still a very young man. According to Church tradition, Joseph was much older than Jesus' mother, Mary, and his death left Jesus, the eldest brother, in charge of the family business.

We know from Scripture that Jesus bar-Joseph was a *tekton* in Greek (see Mark 6:3). A *tekton* was more than just a carpenter. He was a master craftsman who could build a wall or a house, construct a boat, make a table or chair, or throw a bridge across a little stream. Tradition has it that Jesus bar-Joseph specialized in making plows and yokes. I like to imagine that the word around town was that the ox-yokes He made were the best in all of Galilee. Farmers could be certain that if Jesus bar-Joseph made a yoke, it would fit an ox perfectly. There even may have been a sign hanging outside His carpenter shop that read, "My Yoke Is Easy." The word "easy" in the ancient language is *chrestos*, which would be better translated as "well-fitting." In other words, people would be urged to buy their yokes from Jesus bar-Joseph because His yokes fit well. (See Matt. 11:25-30.)

Jesus likely worked in that carpentry shop for years, taking care of His family. Maybe He did so because He knew all too well that before you can attempt the big things—such as being the Savior of the world—you have to take care of the little things, i.e., the everyday obligations of life. The world may call taking care of one's family a "little thing," but it was Jesus' first responsibility. He knew, as He would later teach, that if you are not faithful in little things, you will never be able to do great things (see Matt. 25:22-23).

The day came, however, when Jesus bar-Joseph knew it was time to leave His family and take on the greater mission for which He had been sent into the world. When His mother tried to steer Him (as mothers are known to do) back to a focus on the family, He gently rebuked her (see John 2:4). And later, when His brothers and sisters demanded He give them primary attention, He responded, "Who is my mother, and who are my brothers?" Then, pointing to His disciples, He said, "Here are my mother and my brothers. For whoever does the will of my Father in heaven is my brother and sister and mother" (Matt. 12:48-50).

Jesus bar-Joseph gathered around Himself a small group of followers, and together they proclaimed the Good News that the kingdom of God was at hand—a kingdom that would not come through power, but through sacrificial love. He said that His followers would be drawn to Him because He would one day be lifted up on a cross in an act of sacrificial love for all of humanity. He would draw to Himself a new people who would live out His love in the world (see John 12:30-33). He said that His kingdom would not be *of* the world, even though it would be *in* the world (see John 17:16), and that His weapons, and the weapons used by His followers, would not be the weapons of this world (see 2 Cor. 10:3-4).

Both Jesus bar-Abbas and Jesus bar-Joseph became famous in Judea. Jesus bar-Joseph healed the sick, raised up the lame and made the blind to see—acts of love for a people who longed for God's touch. At the same time, Jesus bar-Abbas used the sword as an instrument of power, using the weapon of the Roman oppressors against them.

The message of Jesus bar-Joseph was a radical leap forward from the teachings of the ancient Jewish prophets and lawgivers. He went beyond their ethical standards and called on people to love their enemies and do good to those who hurt them (see Matt. 5:43-48). He called on people to turn the other cheek, instead of seeking revenge (see Matt. 5:38-42). This Jesus not only upheld the idea that to murder someone was to break the law of Moses, but also taught a higher law that condemned anyone who diminished the dignity of another by calling him a fool (see Matt. 5:21-22).

The new ethic Jesus bar-Joseph declared was a threat to the established social order, which was sustained by power and coercion, and it wasn't long before both political leaders and religious leaders saw how dangerous He was. They said, "If we don't stop Him, the Romans will destroy what is left of our nation" (see John 11:45-53). He stirred up the people and was a disruptive presence from Galilee all the way to Jerusalem (see Luke 23:5). The uneasy détente that the Jewish leaders had established with the Romans was being threatened. Given these realities, they conspired to have Him put to death.

After His arrest on the eve of the Passover feast, Jesus bar-Joseph was beaten and then dragged into Pilate's hall for judgment. Outside the governor's Roman palace, people screamed for His death. The mob had gathered early in the morning at the instigation of the religious and political leaders who wanted Jesus dead.

Pilate, the Roman governor who presided over Israel in those days, could find no evidence against Jesus bar-Joseph that would warrant the death penalty, but the frenzied crowd would settle for nothing less than crucifixion. Knowing it was a Jewish custom at Passover time to pardon a prisoner who had been condemned, he thought there was a way to get out of his predicament. He wanted to avoid, if at all possible, sentencing an innocent man to die.

Pilate sent for another prisoner, one who had been condemned to death by crucifixion on charges of sedition against the Empire and of terrorism, and Jesus bar-Abbas was brought in and made to stand alongside of Jesus bar-Joseph. Pilate must have been confident that, given the choice between the two Jesuses, the people would want Jesus bar-Joseph released rather than the terrorist. *Surely*, he must have said to himself, *they will want this innocent man released and the murderer put to death.* But to Pilate's amazement, when offered the choice between the two would-be saviors, the crowd cried, "Give us bar-Abbas!" Again and again, they screamed for his release.

Then Pilate, like too many politicians down through the ages who have governed based on polls, ignored his conscience. He freed Jesus bar-Abbas and ordered Jesus bar-Joseph, who some called "King of the Jews," to be nailed to a Roman cross.

Today, we are given the same choice that Pilate put before the people on that fateful day. Which Jesus will we choose? Will we choose a Jesus who seeks to establish a kingdom through power and, if need be, violence? Or will we follow the Jesus who calls on us to build the kingdom of God His way: motivated and sustained by sacrificial love?

Too many of us in Christendom, in spite of protests to the contrary, have opted to follow Jesus bar-Abbas. For those who choose the Jesus of power over the Jesus of love, the day will come when we will stand before God's judgment seat and be told, "I don't know you or where you come from. Away from me, all you evildoers!" (Luke 13:27).

Those of us who have followed Jesus bar-Abbas will be confused. What about all the good we accomplished? "But, Lord, we did so many works and wonders in Your name! We built huge cathedrals in Your name. We conquered the armies of sultans and kings in Your name."

And He will say, "You were worshiping the wrong Jesus. You were deluded by power—the greatest delusion of them all."

RULERS IN THE UPSIDE-DOWN KINGDOM

Few things generate more controversy among Christians than political differences (though doctrinal differences are a close second!). Nevertheless, it is essential that any thorough discussion of power give consideration to how Christians should participate in government—or if they should at all.

In 1976, I was a candidate to represent the Fifth District of Pennsylvania to the U.S. Congress. I had a rather simplistic perspective on what was wrong with America, and thought I knew how to straighten out the mess. It seemed to me that the country's problems were a result of having bad people in office, and all that was needed to set things right was to elect good people to replace them. I, of course, considered myself one of the good people.

In the course of formulating this overly simplistic political viewpoint, I failed to ask one question: *Why did politicians in Washington so often fail to uphold the high values and ideals they espoused when they took office?*

In all likelihood, the small number of politicians who betray the trust of the electorate started out as candidates with good motivations. They ran on a platform of integrity and accountability only to later be exposed in their corruption and lies. What went wrong? Why did their sincere and good-hearted dreams die? Why did such hopeful candidates degenerate into political hacks who forgot the good intentions that got them into politics in the first place?

The answer is one word: power.

In politics, it is very difficult to accomplish anything without compromising—and it's very difficult to stay in office without accomplishing anything. (Staying in office is viewed as necessary to accomplish the long-term goals laid out during the candidate's campaign.) It is hard, if not impossible, to work toward policies he believes are right without making concessions to other politicians who promote policies he *doesn't* believe are right. Effective politicians yield on some issues to gain support for others, and constantly have to balance the public good he can do by staying in office with the compromises he must make to keep his job—that is, his or her *power*.

It's just this kind of temptation that leads some politicians to take shortcuts around their values—the very values they so strongly championed when they were candidates! It is a terrible irony.

Prioritizing winning and staying in office over taking principled stands on the issues also sometimes leads to ambiguity. Have you ever noticed, during a forum or debate, that it's sometimes hard to figure out exactly what the candidate is saying? The answers are either so convoluted that you can't nail down his or her position or are so lacking in clarity of conviction that you can't be sure the candidate is telling the truth. Particularly on divisive issues, it's tempting to talk out of both sides of one's mouth in an attempt to gain support from both sides of the argument. For power's sake, a candidate may give a misleading nonanswer, such as "I am personally opposed to abortion, but I question whether there should be a public policy on this matter."

Given how high emotions can run on some topics, it is no wonder that most politicians say no more than is absolutely necessary. They know that no matter how they answer, they will antagonize part of the electorate and diminish their possibilities for staying in power. Too seldom do candidates and politicians answer controversial questions with a simple yes or no, as Jesus commands (see Matt. 5:33-37). For so many, the risks seem too great.

Before taking any position on a controversial issue, a candidate may sometimes poll his constituency in order to gain a clear picture of what stance is favored by likely voters. Instead of basing a decision about a particular issue on his or her personal convictions, the candidate bases them on their popularity with his or her constituency. For instance, a candidate may believe that military spending should be cut and that the monies saved should be used to help the elderly, or to provide support for disabled people, or to establish job-training programs for the unemployed. But if he finds out, through a poll or survey, that his constituents favor an increase in military spending, he may decide to vote their preferences rather than his convictions.

Of course, one might ask if making decisions in this way isn't exactly the right way to do the job. After all, aren't *representatives* elected to *represent* the views, opinions and positions of their constituents?

Personally, I have strong feelings against making policy based solely on what the voters want. When I was a candidate for the U.S. Congress, I was once asked if I would vote in accord with the will of the people in my district. I responded by explaining that, while I would always listen to the voters and learn from them where I might be right and might be wrong, I would, in the end, always vote according to my convictions—even if that meant opposing what the constituents wanted. I would always listen to concerned citizens and be open to changing my mind, but after all was said and done, I would vote according to what I believed was right, even if the people who had elected me had a different opinion.

I went on to recall that when Jesus was on trial, Pilate knew that He was innocent, and even announced to the crowd, "I find no basis for a charge against this man" (Luke 23:4,14). But after careful evaluation of the evidence, Pilate did not move forward with the decision he knew was right. Instead, he took a poll of his constituency.

He asked the crowd, "What shall I do, then, with Jesus who is called Christ?"

The crowd yelled, "Crucify Him!" (See Matt. 27:22.)

And Pilate, endeavoring to pacify the angry mob, voted for the will of the people rather than for the right policy. In order to pacify the people and keep his power, he took a position completely at odds with his conscience—and it cost a man His life.

Needless to say, I lost the election—not for that reason alone, but my views on this matter did not help.

The United States, as we affirm in the Pledge of Allegiance, is a *republic*. In a republic, those elected to office must think through the issues and do what they feel is right for the people. Representatives are expected to vote for the common good as their convictions lead them to an understanding of what policies will best serve the common good. If voters disagree, they can express their displeasure in the next election. *That* is how a democratic republic works.

THE FREEDOM OF THE POWERLESS

Is social change possible without political power and all the compromises that kind of power entails?

In the first chapter of 1 Corinthians, the apostle Paul tells us that God has chosen to change the world through those whom the world considers "foolish" (vv. 18-31). God's choice runs counter to what most people would consider realistic. But as incredible as it may seem, the Scriptures tell us that, through a special kind of human weakness—a weakness that imitates the weakness of Jesus—God is able to do great things (2 Cor. 12:9). The members of the early Church were daring (some might say "foolish") in their willingness to live in joyful abandon in the face of the principalities, powers and rulers of their world—because, for the most part, they had nothing to lose. Having given themselves over to Jesus, what little power, wealth and prestige they possessed were inconsequential. Hence, losing them was not a serious matter. The apostle Paul wrote in Philippians 3:7-8:

> But whatever was to my profit I now consider loss for the sake of Christ. What is more, I consider everything a loss compared to the surpassing greatness of knowing Christ Jesus my Lord, for whose sake I have lost all things. I consider them rubbish, that I may gain Christ.

Christians with that kind of willed weakness or powerlessness can impact society and bring about dramatic social change—and the first-century Christians did! Paul, and others like him who had surrendered without reservation to the will of God, were a threat to the existing social order. They could, and did, become men and women who turned the world upside down.

If we are not conformed to the values of this world, we are free to offer ourselves as "living sacrifices" and are able to live out God's "good, pleasing and perfect will" (Rom. 12:1-2). Totally committed Christians are ready to give up power in favor of love, and they do so without any fear. That is because "perfect love drives out fear" (1 John 4:18).

Powerlessness and fearlessness, rooted in love, make us truly *free*. Those who do not seek power are those most *free* to speak the truth, even when the truth is unpopular. Those who do not crave power are the most *free* to live out faithfulness to God.

A number of years ago, I was asked to deliver an address to a group of political science professors from several Christian colleges. The meeting was held in Washington, DC, and was sponsored by the Council for Christian Colleges and Universities. I chose "Authority and Power in Social Change" as my topic.

I explained to my audience some of what we have already covered in this book: *Power* requires the possibility of using coercive force to make others yield to one's wishes, even against their will; *authority*, on the other hand, is established when someone is able to elicit compliance because others *want* to obey. I explained that with authority, there is no need to control people because they want to do what you ask them to do. If you must resort to power to get others to do what you ask, it may be because you lack authority. I introduced my belief that when power increases, authority generally decreases.

I did not realize it, but in the audience was a political exile from the Philippines. This man, Benigno Aquino, had been a senator and an opposition leader against the near-dictatorial presidency of Ferdinand Marcos. Aquino had been imprisoned in the Philippines because of his outspoken opposition to many of the policies and practices of the Marcos regime, particularly against policies that resulted in the violation of human rights. Marcos had gone so far as to slate Aquino for execution, but Jimmy Carter, then President of the United States, intervened on Aquino's behalf and saved him from death.

The senator was severely ill and would have died in prison had not President Marcos allowed his political prisoner to come to the United States for medical treatment—but only on the condition that Aquino would return to jail in the Philippines following his medical care in a prominent Dallas hospital.

When I met and talked with Aquino after my lecture in Washington, I learned that he had completed the necessary medical treatments and, in accord with his promise, was planning to return in a few weeks to jail in the Philippines. He could have pleaded to stay in the United States as a political refugee but, being a man of honor, he had decided to keep his promise.

I could see that the Filipino leader was thinking about the ideas I had proposed regarding authority and power. When I asked him his thoughts on the lecture, he said, "You have given me hope. I know that when I return to my homeland, I will be powerless, but you have helped me to see that I still can have authority. What I say is right, and the people know it, what I believe to be true. I love my people and I am willing to die for them, and I now believe that if I sacrifice my personal safety I will have great influence in the Philippines, even though I will have no power at all."

When he returned to the Philippines, Aquino was assassinated. Before he even got off the airplane, an assassin in the uniform of Marcos's military shot him to death.

That, however, is not the end of the story. Benigno Aquino was right! When this Christian brother presented himself as a "living sacrifice" for justice, he gained authority. And although he was dead, his movement for justice and freedom, based on his loving sacrifice, gained momentum. The opposition party grew from a small minority to a vast crusade, ending in the ouster of Ferdinand Marcos and the election of Corazon Aquino, Benigno's wife, to the Filipino presidency. Until that day, the opposition party, inspired by Benigno Aquino's example, protested the oppressive regime by taking to the streets non-violently and in prayer. When Marcos and his notorious wife, Imelda, fled the country, freedom and democracy won in a bloodless coup. In presenting himself as a living, loving sacrifice, Aquino changed the destiny of a nation—not by wielding power, but by laying down his life.

As a sociologist, I am constantly confronted by those who contend that, without power, positive social change is an impossibility. In response,

I always point out that in recent times, the most significant social changes have been wrought by people who wielded no political power at all. Neither Mahatma Gandhi nor Martin Luther King, Jr., ever held political office. Neither of them commanded an army. Yet history attests to the effectiveness of these men in inspiring sweeping social change.

Those who are crucified for righteousness' sake shall rise again because there is no power on earth that can bury those who live out sacrificial love. Easter is evidence that the principalities and powers of this world will never have the last word. That is because the One who suffered in weakness and rose again from the dead, along with those who follow His example, will triumph. As Handel expressed it in his now-famous "Hallelujah" chorus, inspired by the book of Revelation: "The kingdoms of this world will become the kingdom of our Lord and of His Christ. And He shall reign forever and ever. Hallelujah! Hallelujah!" (see Rev. 11:15; 19:6).

The greatest changes in history have come about not through power, but through those who have gained authority through sacrificial love and become agents of God through whom all principalities, powers, dominions and thrones will be brought into subjection to God's will (see Eph. 1:19-23). Those who turn from power to sacrificial love may lose many battles along the way, but they lose those battles for a cause that ultimately triumphs—which is much better than winning battles for a cause that ultimately fails!

THE DANGERS OF ABANDONING POLITICAL POWER

The Amish, some Mennonites and others who are part of the Anabaptist tradition have concluded that Christians ought not hold political office. Many of these brothers and sisters even refuse to vote. They reason that Christians should never exercise power or coerce others to do what is right—and that voting is a kind of power. In a radical disengagement from the principalities and powers of this world, some Anabaptists have sought not to be citizens of this world, but instead to live as loyal citizens of God's kingdom. While paying their taxes and obeying the laws of the state, they nevertheless have rejected their "rights" to exercise power within the worldly domain.

It might seem reasonable to conclude, from all I have already said, that I agree with my Anabaptist friends. On one hand, I do. But on the other, I do not. Allow me to explain—and I will do my best to avoid talking out of both sides of my mouth, like some of the politicians that I have criticized!

What Amish and some Mennonite friends believe about being citizens of another kingdom—the kingdom of God—is true. Christians should not see ourselves primarily as citizens of this world, but recognize that we Christians belong to another kingdom. In accord with what the apostle Paul wrote in Ephesians 2:19, Anabaptists see themselves as fellow citizens with the saints in "God's household" and, as Paul wrote in 2 Corinthians 5:20, as ambassadors to this world from Christ's kingdom. Christians from other traditions would do well to follow the Anabaptist's lead and remember where our allegiance lies. Before we are Americans, Canadians, Kenyans or Pakistanis, we are the Family of God.

Nevertheless, I believe that becoming involved in politics is something Christians must do in this day and age. I recognize the compromise with the world that politics involves and realize that holding political office, in particular, can provide a terrible temptation to grasp at power. But I also think that it may be irresponsible and dangerous for God's world if Christians, in an effort to stand clear of political process and remain uncontaminated by involvement in politics, allow the unchallenged election of candidates who might do harm to society and oppress the innocent.

France's first president in the post-World War II era, General Charles de Gaulle, once said, "Politics are too serious a matter to be left to politicians." I tend to agree. I also resonate with Edmund Burke's oft-quoted observation: "All that is necessary for the triumph of evil is that good men do nothing." I am convinced that dedicated Christians must recognize the importance of their influence on the world God created and longs to redeem. The alternative—that good Christians do nothing—means nothing less than handing the world over to evil.

Humanity is sinful. People are motivated by the lusts of the flesh. There are destructive tendencies in all of us. In the face of such facts, God has given us rulers to govern us with justice, to protect us from humanity's worst tendencies (see Rom. 13:2-3). Recognizing what is at stake, Christians should not avoid political responsibilities, but should hold power with reluctance. Plato spoke the truth when he proposed that only someone who does not desire power is fit to hold it.[1] If we are truly seeking to imitate Christ, we do not desire power—thus making Christians fit to hold power when justice demands it.

Of course, Christians who heed the call to political involvement—whether by voting or by running for office—must be vigilant against the corrupting influence of power. We should see political power as an unfortunate necessity, given that we live in a fallen world where evil must be constrained and punished. But we must take care lest the power we are given gains power over us.

The Cultural Imperative

Because of what political power can do to those who possess it, some contemporary Reformed theologians have recognized the need for Christians to enter politics, and have called on Christian citizens to exercise checks and controls over those in public office. Acting from John Calvin's "cultural imperative," many Reformed Christians believe that God wills for them to invade every sector of society and culture and endeavor to bring all things under the Lordship of Christ. To them, this means that Christians must enter the political arena with the explicit purpose of transforming government into the kind of system God wills for it to be. They also believe that Christians must never relinquish the right to serve as a conscience to those who do take up positions of power. There is, however, a big difference between being the conscience of the state and trying to control the state. I believe that this is a distinction that is too often forgotten by Christians who are passionate about political action, whether on the Right or the Left.

Because they control thousands of radio stations and have an extensive presence on religious television programming, the Religious Right often comes across as the public persona of all Christianity. The general public is sometimes frightened by what comes across the airwaves, and leaps to the conclusion that all Evangelicals hold views that seem anti-gay, anti-feminist, anti-environmentalist, pro-war and supportive of the gun lobby. In short, they are often viewed as the radical right of the Republican Party at Prayer. I strongly believe that Christians who become involved in politics should not act in a totally partisan manner—otherwise, being a Christian too easily becomes equated with being Republican. God is not a Republican.

I also want to emphasize that God is not a Democrat, either. The tendency of Christians on the Left to make God into an expression of liberal political ideologies is a very serious mistake. In our political involvements, we must always make it clear that the God that we worship transcends partisan politics and will bring judgment on all parties whenever they deviate from the love and justice mandated in the Bible. The great playwright George Bernard Shaw once said, "God created man in His image and then man returned the favor." Sadly, that is all too true. We must make every effort to keep from defining God as the legitimizer of any human-made political ideology.

Christians are free to (and should) partner with any and every political party that they believe seeks to govern with justice. We are called by Jesus to be "the salt of the earth" (Matt. 5:13). In ancient times, salt was used as a preservative to keep food from spoiling. Thus, we can interpret the words of Jesus to mean that we should be a people who permeate every sector of society, including the political sector, in order to counteract the corrupting influences of the evil one. Jesus also told us that we were to be "leaven" (see Matt. 13:33). Even as leaven has a transforming effect on dough, we are called to have a transforming effect within all of society, and, in this case, within a political process.

But we should not strive to control any party or use any party to impose our will on others. To exercise political responsibility, Christians must learn what issues are facing the nation at election time and reflect on those issues in light of the Bible's teaching. Theologian Karl Barth recommended holding a Bible in one hand and a newspaper in the other. It bothers me when I hear a Christian say, "I am not concerned with politics because I am too committed to spiritual things." We must not be politically ignorant or indifferent. All the world belongs to the Lord—there is no sector of society that should be excluded from our concern. Jesus commanded us to go into all the world to declare the gospel, and the political arena is part of that world (see Matt. 28:16-20).

WARNINGS TO THE REST OF US

We should be aware that those who rule over us possess the potential to do us harm by using their power in oppressive ways. In the Hebrew Bible, God told the children of Israel that they would be better off without a king and urged them to let YHWH be their ruler. YHWH was well aware that He alone could be trusted with power and be able to resist its corrupting influence. He told the children of Israel that if they had a king like the other nations of the world—which is what they desired—

their king would oppress them and reduce them to slavery. We read in Scripture:

> Samuel told all the words of the LORD to the people who were asking him for a king. He said, "This is what the king who will reign over you will do: He will take your sons and make them serve with his chariots and horses, and they will run in front of his chariots. Some he will assign to be commanders of thousands and commanders of fifties, and others to plow his ground and reap his harvest, and still others to make weapons of war and equipment for his chariots. He will take your daughters to be perfumers and cooks and bakers. He will take the best of your fields and vineyards and olive groves and give them to his attendants. He will take a tenth of your grain and of your vintage and give it to his officials and attendants. Your menservants and maidservants and the best of your cattle and donkeys he will take for his own use. He will take a tenth of your flocks, and you yourselves will become his slaves. When that day comes, you will cry out for relief from the king you have chosen, and the LORD will not answer you in that day" (1 Sam. 8:10-18).

Unfortunately, the children of Israel did not heed the pleadings of YHWH and continued to implore God for a king. Having a king, they felt, would give them prestige—they wanted the same symbols of power enjoyed by other nations. Eventually, YHWH gave in to their pleadings and gave them what they wanted. Sadly, it was only a matter of time before the people of Israel experienced the trials and tribulations of which YHWH had warned them. As we read through the Scriptures, we find that even the best of Israel's kings could not resist the corrupting effects of power.

There was King Saul, who so longed to hold on to power that he was ready to destroy the one whom God had appointed to be his successor. Eventually, Saul sought out the services of a witch to find out if he would survive as Israel's ruler, so great was his hunger to remain in power (see 1 Sam. 28:7-25).

Consider King Solomon, who began his reign with the best of intentions by asking God for wisdom so that he might rule over his people with justice. Yet in spite of his wonderful beginning, Solomon used his power to appease his lust for women. As king, he had the power to get everything he wanted—and he used people for his own gratification. In the end, his abuse of power destroyed him (see 1 Kings 11).

David, Saul's successor and Solomon's father, is considered by many to have been the best of Israel's kings—yet he also let power get the best of him. One day, while his nation was at war, King David was on the balcony of his palace when his eyes fell upon Bathsheba, a beautiful woman married to Uriah, a general who was away serving David's army on the battlefield. David burned with sexual desire when he saw Bathsheba taking a bath. Because he was the absolute monarch in Israel and could do what he pleased without restraint, he decided to gratify his appetites and have sexual relations with Bathsheba. The pregnancy that resulted from this adulterous relationship led David to execute a devious plan. The king called Uriah back from the battlefield and tried to induce him to enjoy sexual pleasures with his wife so that the pregnancy could be attributed to him. The plan went awry, however. As a faithful soldier, Uriah thought it would be wrong to sleep with his wife while the soldiers who served under him risked their lives in battle.

David's schemes then became even more sinister. He sent Uriah back into battle with instructions from the king to his superior officer that Uriah should be ordered to the thick of the fighting, where he was certain to be killed (see 2 Sam. 11). David's unchecked power tempted him not only to commit adultery but also murder.

Stories like these have played out down through the ages. The chronicles of history are littered with accounts of those who sought power with a promise, and even with the intention to use it for good once it had been secured. But in case after case, we know of rulers who turned to tyranny and oppression to consolidate for themselves the power they promised to use on behalf of the people. Even today, we see the succession of revolts and coups in unstable developing nations. Revolutionary leaders challenge established totalitarian regimes with promises of freedom. Once they are in power, however, the only significant change, in most cases, seems to be the color of the palace guards' uniforms.

According to Georg Sorel, one of the seminal thinkers in the field of sociology, this is inevitable. Sorel pointed out that when revolutionaries rise to power, they have no choice but to violently suppress those whom they just overthrew. They are constantly aware that the previous political-military order, after having been defeated, has not simply faded away. It lurks in the shadows, waiting to take power back when an opportunity presents itself. The revolutionaries, now in power by way of violence, depend on continued violence to keep the previous rulers from reasserting themselves.[2]

We have all heard the leaders of liberation movements make promises of peace and freedom once the oppressive governments they challenged were ousted from power. Then, sadly, we have watched the new rulers exercise even greater excesses of tyranny and oppression than the ones that preceded them. Friedrich Nietzsche once said, "Be careful when you fight the monsters, lest you become one." Those who have sought to eliminate abusive political leaders with the use of violent power usually become just like those whom they once challenged.

Christians with a biblically based view of human nature understand the inherent tendency that all people have to abuse power. Hence, many

Christians tend to be politically cautious, "conservative" in the classical sense of the word. Conservatives recognize that human beings cannot be trusted with power. They are afraid to give government too much power; they are skeptical that government can do as much good as liberals believe. They are never completely convinced by even the most well-meaning aspirants to political office, who promise to make the world a better place (if only they are given the power to do so).

The United States government was designed by men who shared this biblical understanding of human nature that those who have unchecked power cannot be trusted with it. That is why the U.S. Constitution outlines a system whereby no branch of government can exercise unlimited power. The president cannot do much without the consent of Congress and the actions of Congress can be vetoed by the president. Both Congress and the president can be restrained by decisions of the Supreme Court. The founders of our nation, impacted by a biblical view of human nature, were determined not to allow themselves to fall under the control of an absolute ruler, no matter how good the intentions of that ruler might be. Remembering the monarchs who ruled throughout the Europe they had fled, the founders of our nation were determined to give absolute power to no one.

THE LIMITS OF GOVERNMENT POWER

Even as Christians become involved with politics, we should remember what government can and cannot do. Government is ordained by God to restrain evil (see Rom. 13), but it cannot do everything. Over the past several years, many within the U.S. government have recognized this fact and, on a bipartisan basis, have established partnerships with faith-based groups. Government has recognized that such groups can render necessary services to the neediest people in society more efficiently and with less expense than the government can. I believe that these partnerships have significant possibilities for extending the good work that God has called us to do in the world.

I have heard some say that the government ought to keep out the problems of the poor—that dealing with these concerns is the sole prerogative of the Church. Indeed, there is no question that the Church has vast resources, which, if mobilized to minister to the poor, might accomplish a great deal. But when we turn our gaze globally, especially to the developing world, we have to recognize that the Church alone cannot resolve the problems. To eliminate poverty in the poorest regions on earth, infrastructure is needed—such things as roads and airports, sewage treatment systems and power systems. Building infrastructure of this kind falls within the jurisdiction of government, not the Church. There is much we can do, but there are some things that must be left in the hands of the state. I believe that God is able to accomplish what needs to be done, not only through the Church, but through the government as well. The government can become an instrument used by God. The book of Colossians suggests that this principality and power was explicitly created to accomplish such ends (see Col. 1:16).

The Church is the Body of Christ, and as such is called to continue the work Jesus began while He was here on earth. The Spirit that was alive in Jesus should be alive in each and every member of the Church, enabling us together to continue His work. There is no question that the Church is called to not only win the lost, but also to serve the poor and the needy—just as Jesus did.

Eastern University, the Christian school where I teach, has many students who are committed to serving the needs of some of Philadelphia's poorest people. In one low-cost housing development, a group of dedicated young people took over many of the social services previously carried out by city social workers. They ran summer camps; established a variety of social clubs for teenagers; initiated job placement programs for adults; developed a tenants' council to enable community members to make decisions that determine their social destinies; provided counseling and juvenile protection for delinquent youth; and developed an array of evangelistic programs that reach the people of the community with the message of Christ. This is the Church at work in the world.

Some churches have done heroic things. I know of a church in suburban Philadelphia that, during the Civil Rights era, became concerned about African-American brothers and sisters living in the Philly ghetto. After much debate and struggle, the church members decided to mortgage their building and make those funds available to meet emergency needs in the inner city.

The church went into debt for $150,000. With those funds, the church was able to invest in a variety of programs in African-American churches that did not have the means to do the things they had wanted to do for the poor in their neighborhoods. Daycare centers, reading clinics, thrift shops, job placement programs and assistance to the elderly all became a reality within a few months.

What was amazing was the response of the media in the greater Philadelphia area. Newspapers carried full-page stories and television stations reported on the commitment of this suburban church and its accomplishments during spots on the evening news. Later, two national magazines covered the story.

At first, I couldn't understand why such a fuss was being made, but little by little I realized that when the Church stops talking about being the servant of God and becomes the servant of God, *it is news!* Nobody is surprised when a church takes on a mortgage to improve its facilities or to put up a new building; people expect the Church to aggrandize its own stature and to provide for its own people. What amazes the world is when a church is willing to sacrifice itself and its resources for the welfare of others, when it expresses love with no thought of return.

Of course, that's what it means to do the work of God in the world. But there are limits to what the Church as a social institution can do to bring about the justice and wellbeing of society. Christians cannot solely do all the things that must be done to make something of God's will to be done "on earth as it is in heaven." We must humbly realize that God is at work outside the Church, and we Christians should seek to discern what God is doing in the world and join those efforts. I believe that God is at work through governments to stop environmental degradation, eliminate racial discrimination, curtail sexism, work for peace, protect the poor, and a host of other initiatives designed to move society toward what God wants it to be.

Many of us believe that to think that the Church has the resources and the will to meet even the minimal needs of the elderly poor, provide the basic health needs of the uninsured, pay for adequate care of those disabled persons with special needs, and establish the wide range of educational programs required for our advanced technological society—without extensive governmental involvement—is unrealistic. Those of us who believe this way contend that we need for government to do what the institutional Church cannot do. But even as we work within the framework of government, we must always be on guard against government becoming "Big Brother" and curtailing our lives.

WHAT TO DO WHILE WE WAIT FOR THE SECOND COMING

No consideration of the role Christians should play in government would be complete without some discussion about civil disobedience. During the days of Hitler's regime, some German Christians believed it was wrong to oppose the government, despite its obvious immorality. Their religious duty was to obey "the higher powers." They believed that God would not hold them responsible for what the government did or ordered them to do.

There are many who categorically answer the question with a no. They claim that Romans 13 leaves no room for civil disobedience and that the apostle Paul teaches us to view government leaders as ministers of God, regardless how evil they or their policies are. These fellow believers claim that if we obey unjust laws or rulers and evil results, we are not to blame; God will judge the rulers rather than judging us.

I must admit that such a position has much to commend itself. It is a neat and explicit doctrine based on a straightforward interpretation of Paul's writings to the Romans. It also places the responsibility for our government's morality on shoulders other than our own, the loss of which burden is a relief. However, over the last couple of decades, my thinking on this subject has shifted away from an interpretation of Scripture that condemns all forms of civil disobedience.

I once was asked to deliver a series of lectures for "Spiritual Emphasis Week" at a small church-related college. I had just finished giving what I thought was a thorough explanation of a Christian view of government, when a sophomoric-looking young man rose to his feet and asked, "Mr. Preacher, what ideas have you got about civil disobedience?"

The question was relevant to the times. It was the early 1960s and the Civil Rights movement was in high gear. Many of its leaders advocated civil disobedience to call attention to the segregation and discrimination that African-American people had to endure. By disobeying the laws and being arrested, many African-Americans felt that they could demonstrate the injustice of the Jim Crow system. However, many sincere conservatives believed the civil disobedience would lead to a breakdown of law and order, and would lead to the end of the social contract that makes government possible. At that time, I listed myself among the law-and-order advocates and responded to the student's question by reading to him from Romans 13:

> Everyone must submit himself to the governing authorities, for there is no authority except that which God has established. The authorities that exist have been established by God. Consequently, he who rebels against the authority is rebelling against what God has instituted, and those who do so will bring judgment on themselves (vv. 1-2).

"Does that answer your question?" I asked.

"Not really," he answered with a nasal Southern accent that evoked in me a sense that I was dealing with a hillbilly just waiting to be demolished. I viewed people with accents or twangs in their speech as unsophisticated down-home folk who may have had some crackerjack wisdom, but who were out of touch with the intellectual exchange of the Eastern establishment (of which I foolishly considered myself a part). Such *a priori* assumptions, I learned, can prove disastrous.

"Where was Paul when he wrote that stuff?" asked my inquisitor.

I gulped and answered with a somewhat embarrassed air, "In jail."

I cleared my throat to indicate that I wanted to move on, but he came back again with another question: "How did he get in jail?"

I responded that it was a long story and not too relevant to present-day civil disobedience. He ignored my response and gave his own explanation: "Let me tell you how Paul got there. You see, Preacher, they were having problems with race relations down there in Jerusalem. The Gentiles and the Jews weren't getting along. They had separate churches, probably because the Gentiles had a different kind of music, were loud and shouted 'Amens' during the sermon. It could be the Jews were into dignity and good music and that kind of stuff. I'm really not sure what the problem was, but they just weren't getting along. Some of the big preachers in the Early Church thought they ought to hold a conference to see whether this segregation was a good thing or a bad thing. They invited old Paul to come to the meeting, and Paul said to himself, *I oughta go to that meeting to show them people that Jesus don't tolerate no divisions that separate different kinds of folks and that He came to make everybody one.* Paul knew that talkin' usually doesn't do no good. You gotta *show* people what's right. So old Paul, he got himself a Gentile friend and decided that the two of them would go down to Jerusalem together and show them other apostles that Jesus puts together people who the world tries to keep apart. You can read all about it, Preacher, in the book of Acts."

I felt the crowd slipping away from me. The young man was getting the upper hand and I didn't know how to stop him. He just went on and on.

"Jews and Gentiles didn't travel together in them days. When they went any place on a boat, they stayed in separate compartments. I think Gentiles sat in the back of the boat; but old Paul wouldn't have none of it. He traveled with that Gentile just like he was his own brother. They rode together all the way to Jerusalem. I don't know what you call that, Preacher, but it sounds like the first Freedom Ride to me.

"When they got down there to Jerusalem, Paul knew that the rules of the city said that Gentiles and Jews shouldn't eat together, especially in a public place. That sounds like a stupid rule to us, but them Jews were serious about that stuff. They ate in segregated restaurants and wouldn't put up with anything else. Old Paul wasn't going to tolerate such foolishness, so he found himself a public eating place, and he and his Gentile friend sat themselves down and had a feast, right where everybody could see. It must have upset a lot of people, but Paul didn't care 'cause he was staging the first sit-in. You can read about it in the book of Acts, about in chapter 21."

The crowd was giggling and I was shrinking. My questioner had a smirk on his face. "It didn't end there," he said. "After they finished, Paul decided to head up to the Temple. What denomination are you, Preacher?" he asked.

"Baptist," I responded tersely.

"Well, let's say it was the Baptist temple they went to. They were about halfway down the street when the people realized where they were going. Paul was going to take that Gentile man into the holy place in the Temple and people from the Gentile race weren't allowed in there! Now it's one thing to have a Freedom Ride and it's another thing to have a sit-in; but old Paul was about to stage the first *pray*-in. He was gonna take that man from the other race right into that segregated temple. That was really something. The Jews weren't about to put up with that stuff, and they jumped all over Paul and his friend and beat them to the ground. There was a regular riot going on. You can read about it in the book of Acts. Now, Preacher, if Paul was really a man of God, what was he doing in a race riot? That's what I'd like to know."

The crowd's giggles had turned to laughter, but that down-homer wasn't finished with me yet.

"You know they would've killed old Paul except for the police who happened to show up just in time. They took Paul into what we call 'protective custody.' When they got Paul and his Gentile friend down to the jailhouse, they decided to beat them up. Police don't like troublemakers no matter what they stand for. I guess you can say they exercised a little 'police brutality'—until they heard Paul was a Roman citizen. It's all there in the book of Acts."

I knew he was moving in for the kill, but there was no stopping him now: "The next day, they brought old Paul up for a hearing before the authorities and Paul broke the news to them. He said, 'You guys picked on the wrong polecat. You may not know it, but I'm a Roman citizen and I got rights. You probably thought I was just one of them unregistered voters that politicians can just ignore.'

"Well, when the authorities heard that, they were plenty scared. They tried to get old Paul to forget the whole thing and leave town by sundown. But Paul wasn't going to let them get off so easy. There was a principle at stake and he had a point to make. He said, 'No way are you gonna get by easy on this one. I'm appealing this case. I'm taking it to the Supreme Court.' Now, in them days, the Supreme Court was in Rome, so Paul said, 'I'm going to Rome and let them people in Caesar's palace hand down a ruling on me and what I'm doing.' He figured that he had broken the rules of Jerusalem, but that the people up there in the Supreme Court would declare those rules stupid and unconstitutional.

"It was while he was on his way to Rome that Paul wrote a letter to the Romans. You recited part of that letter, the part where he said, 'Be subject to the higher powers.' Seems funny that he should say that after all he did. If you ask me, Paul figured it was okay to break some laws if the laws made you do stuff that was against the will of God. You probably don't agree with that, Preacher. You probably don't agree with that at all."

I was trapped. I knew it, and he knew it. Worst of all, the crowd knew it. And while he may have jumbled up some of the facts of the story, there was no denying that he knew the principles inherent in that passage of Romans. Quite well, in fact.

A POSSIBLE PARADOX

There comes a time when the dictates of the ruling authorities must be opposed because to obey the commands of the state would make one unfaithful to the commands of the Lord. The question that lies before us at such times is how one can resist the power of government and still be faithful to the commandments of Scripture as outlined in the thirteenth chapter of Romans.

Apostles Peter and John faced a situation in which the rulers of Israel commanded them to refrain from preaching about Jesus (see Acts 4:13-20). When they had to decide whether to obey the officials of the state or be faithful to the command to preach the gospel, these early disciples chose to disobey the civil authorities. We read:

> But Peter and John replied, "Judge for yourselves whether it is right in God's sight to obey you rather than God. For we cannot help speaking about what we have seen and heard" (Acts 4:19-20).

I believe that it is possible to practice civil disobedience *and* simultaneously obey the command of Scripture to be subject to the authority of the state, even when what the state orders violates the Christian conscience. This paradox is possible because the government always gives people two alternatives. Those two alternatives are: *Do what we tell you* or *Submit to our punishment.* Down through the ages, Christians have at times found it necessary to refuse to obey the government, but when they disobeyed, they usually submitted to the government's punishment for their disobedience. This may seem like a strange way of submitting, but I believe it's an honest way of submitting. It recognizes the right of government to exercise power over its subjects, while at the same time providing a way for those subjects not to capitulate when obedience would require a compromise of convictions.

In the earliest days of Church history, Christians felt that bowing down before the statue of Caesar would be disobeying the First Commandment. They believed that an act of homage and worship to Caesar would betray the Scriptures that commanded them to offer such worship to none other but God. Forced by conscience to disobey the command to worship Caesar, Christians accepted the second alternative provided by the government: They submitted themselves for punishment, even when that punishment meant being thrown to the lions or slain by gladiators.

Martin Luther King, Jr. faced that same dilemma during the years of the Civil Rights movement. He went into many communities to protest unjust laws that discriminated against his African-American brothers and sisters. In his opposition to such laws, he often found it necessary to practice civil disobedience. When he did, he presented himself for arrest. In so doing, he obeyed Scripture's mandate to submit himself to government.

During the years of the Vietnam War, a similar dilemma presented itself to many Christian young people. Those who were opposed to their country's involvement in the war felt that they could not, in clear conscience, participate as soldiers. Many of these young people also rejected any role as army medics. They believed that by taking such positions they were only releasing other military personnel to unjustly do battle with the Vietnamese. When they were drafted, a number of these young people fled across the border into Canada or went to live in Europe to escape military service. I felt (and still feel) that fleeing the country was a refusal to submit to higher authorities. It would have been better for these young people to present themselves to the civil authorities for arrest. In so doing, they would have been subject to the government and would, at the same time, have pricked the conscience of the nation. Imagine thousands of our finest young men behind bars during the Vietnam years because they could not in clear conscience participate in a war they believed contrary to the will of God. Such action would have caused us to ask important questions much earlier than we did, and the sufferings of untold thousands might have been prevented.

I am not necessarily suggesting that those opposed to the war in Vietnam were right in what they believed; I am only endeavoring to outline the proper way for Christians to exercise opposition to a government committed to action they deem opposed to God's will.

Dietrich Bonhoeffer presents to us a case wherein a man of conscience found it necessary to stand against the ruling authority, who in this case was Adolph Hitler. When war broke out in Germany, Bonhoeffer's homeland, he was serving as a faculty member at Union Theological Seminary in New York City. His friend and colleague Reinhold Niebuhr urged him to stay in America, but Bonhoeffer believed that he would have no *authority* to speak in Germany after the war if he did not suffer with the German people under the evil Nazi dictator raising havoc in his homeland. So Bonhoeffer went home, just as thousands of others sought to flee.

Things in Germany went from bad to worse, and there came a point where Bonhoeffer knew that Hitler had to be stopped by any means necessary, lest all of Europe be completely destroyed. He said, "If I see a madman driving a car into a group of innocent bystanders, then I can't, as a

Christian, simply wait for the catastrophe and then comfort the wounded and bury the dead. I must try to wrestle the steering wheel out of the hands of the driver."

Bonhoeffer joined with a small group that plotted to assassinate Hitler. As the plan unfolded, a bomb was carried into a room where Hitler met with some of his advisors. The bomb was detonated. It killed and wounded several in the room, but Adolph Hitler came away with only very superficial scratches. Not long after, Bonhoeffer, along with his fellow conspirators, was hunted down and put in a concentration camp. He was put to death just prior to the camp's liberation by Allied forces.

Did Bonhoeffer do the right thing in his attempt to kill Hitler? Had he succeeded, millions of lives might have been saved. But is murder ever justified?

Here is a sad irony: Bonhoeffer, in his deep commitment to the teachings of Jesus in the Sermon on the Mount, was a pacifist. Thus, his actions ran contrary to his convictions about using violence to do good. He admitted later that he had entered into the plot because of a lack of faith in God. If his faith had been stronger, Bonhoeffer contended, he would not have resorted to means that were contrary to the teachings of Christ.

Dietrich Bonhoeffer's story demonstrates that there is no easy answer to questions about power, violence and civil disobedience.

POWER IN A NUCLEAR AGE

We live in one of the most threatening times in human history. An increasing number of nations have nuclear weapons at their disposal. Even more frightening is the strong possibility, if not a probability, that nuclear weapons might fall into the hands of terrorist groups. While researching this subject, I have discovered that significant amounts of enriched uranium and plutonium that were once in the hands of the Soviet Union are presently unaccounted for. Beyond that, many nuclear weapons in nations that were once part of the Soviet Bloc are so poorly guarded that they could easily be stolen. In at least two places, nuclear weapons capable of destroying entire cities were guarded by only a few soldiers outside an anchor wire fence![1]

Yet in the face of these very real threats, the Church has had very little to say against weapons of mass destruction. As a matter of fact, several American Evangelical denominations applaud nuclear weapons and see them as a deterrent to war. They believe that building such bombs is a way of making peace.

Those of us who call for nuclear disarmament are sometimes viewed as spiritually suspect by some of our Evangelical brothers and sisters, as strange as that may sound. For these folks, Christianity is deeply entwined with American nationalism. They contend that the militaristic posture of America is somehow God-ordained, and assume that those who reject nuclear weapons are somehow unfaithful to the teachings of Christ. Such thinking is convoluted, but the fact remains that there are some who believe that building a nuclear arsenal is a reasonable, and even Christian, thing to promote.

Presently, the United States is working hard to keep nations such as North Korea and Iran from developing nuclear weapons. Our former president declared North Korea and Iran to be part of an "axis of evil" that had to be destroyed. Hearing such a bellicose statement, it is not surprising to me that these nations should look on America as a threat; and because atomic weapons, according to us, are the only deterrent against a nuclear attack, the development of such weapons may seem to be the only way to ensure their own survival.

I don't think that the United States will be able to convince Iran and North Korea to forgo membership in the "nuclear power club" so long as our nation remains a member. Can we expect other nations to melt down their nuclear weapons when we are unwilling to do so?

There are still those who talk about the possibility of "winning" a nuclear war. They talk about "acceptable levels" of deaths, pointing out that it is possible to wage a nuclear war in which "only" one hundred million Americans lose their lives. Such "optimistic" projections of survival do not take into consideration warnings from some of the most outstanding spokespersons of the medical profession. Doctors tell us that, for those who survive a nuclear war, life would be all but unbearable. Large proportions of the population would suffer from radiation that would cause them to vomit to death, while others would have cancer growing in their bodies at a fantastically high speed. Still others would suffer such emotional and psychological shock that normal life would be impossible.

Nevertheless, those who strategize nuclear warfare claim that such people can be called "winners." Hopefully, say these planners of World War III, the destruction wrought among our enemies would be so much greater that we could be deemed the victors. Talk like this makes us aware of the absurdities of power and the callousness it creates among those who possess it.

In light of the horrendous prospects of nuclear war, some few respected Evangelical leaders have become what can be called "nuclear pacifists." Billy Graham has been quoted as saying, "The present arms race is a terrifying thing, and it is almost impossible to overestimate its potential for disaster. . . . Is nuclear holocaust inevitable if the arms race is not stopped? Frankly, the answer is almost certainly yes."[2]

John Stott, Rector Emeritus of All Souls Church in London, has said, "Because [nuclear weapons] are indiscriminate in their effects, destroying combatants and non-combatants alike, it seems clear to me that they are ethically indefensible, and that every Christian, whatever he or she may think of the possibility of a 'just' use of conventional weapons, must be a nuclear pacifist."[3]

For the first time in many years, peacemaking is no longer the sole prerogative of people who can easily be ignored as left-wingers or "pinkos."

Other leading Evangelicals such as Jim Wallis of the Sojourners community and Vernon Grounds, President Emeritus of the Conservative Baptist Theological Seminary in Denver, Colorado, have called for a conference on "The Church and Peacemaking in the Nuclear Age." Joining them are leaders of most mainline denominations, which believe that the military power of the dominant nations of the world has reached such incredible dimensions that it requires opposition from all who are concerned about life on this planet.

Peacemaking is risky. We know that to be true when we look at the cross and see what they did to the ultimate peacemaker in human history. Peacemaking requires faith and faith demands risk-taking. But people of faith know that only if the people of God are willing to take risks is there any hope for the world. To be peacemakers may mean being persecuted for righteousness' sake. It may involve having the so-called realists of the world call us foolish. But then, the way of Christ has always been foolishness to those who are not of the mind of Christ (see 1 Cor. 1:18).

JUST WAR THEORY

It used to be that many theologians and philosophers supported the case for what is called the "just war theory," which says that there are certain conditions under which a Christian might be justified in going to war. In Everett L. Long's book *War and Conscience in America*, he explains the just war position. Ronald Sider and Richard Taylor summarize and elaborate on Long's explanation in their important book *Nuclear Holocaust and Christian Hope*. It is worth our time and consideration to set forth the characteristics of a just war at this point in our discussion.

1. *Last resort*. "All other means to the morally just solution of a conflict must be exhausted before resort to arms can be re-

garded as legitimate." War must be the last resort, but that does not mean that an unjust solution must be accepted.

2. *Just cause.* "War can be just only if employed to defend a stable order or morally preferable cause against threats of destruction or the use of injustice." The goals for which one fights must be just. And the opponent must be clearly unjust, even though one recognizes moral ambiguity even in oneself.

3. *Right attitudes.* "War must be carried out with the right attitudes." The intention must be the restoration of justice, not retaliation. Anger and revenge have no part in just wars.

4. *Prior declaration of war.* "War must be explicitly declared by a legitimate authority." Individual citizens must not take up arms as self-appointed defenders of justice. A formal declaration of war must precede armed conflict so that the opponent has an opportunity to abandon unjust activities and prevent war.

5. *Reasonable hope of success.* "War may be conducted only by military means that promise a reasonable attainment of the moral and political objectives being sought." If there is not a reasonable chance of success, then it is wrong to fight, no matter how just one's cause. Nor does this simply mean that one must *think* one can win; there must be a reasonable probability that the things for which one is fighting will not be destroyed in the process.

6. *Noncombatant immunity.* "The just war theory has also entailed selective immunity for certain parts of the enemy's population, particularly for noncombatants." Noncombatants

are all those not directly involved in the manufacture, direction or use of weapons. In a just war, no military action may be aimed directly at noncombatants. That is not to say that civilians may never be injured. If an army justly destroys a military target and nearby noncombatants are killed, that is an unintended side effect (called "double effect"), which is permissible within limits. But the principle of proportionality applies here.

7. *Proportionality.* Finally, the principle of proportionality specifies that there must be a reasonable expectation that the good results of the war will exceed the horrible evils involved. This principle applies both to the whole enterprise of the war and to specific tactics in the course of battle. For example, if the unintended double effect of attacking a legitimate military target involves killing a disproportionate number of noncombatants, then the action is immoral.[4]

Obviously, the conditions of a just war cannot be met in a nuclear holocaust. First, in nuclear warfare, prior declaration of war is totally impossible; a basic condition for "winning" a nuclear war is to engage in a surprise attack whereby enemy rockets and bombs are put out of commission. Second, there is no reasonable hope for success in a nuclear war because even the winners are fantastic losers; the nation and the people for whom the war is fought suffer irreparable damage. Third, there is no way noncombatants can be immune from the destruction of a nuclear battle. Finally, there is no way to say that the good that might result from such a war would outweigh the evil that would result from a failure to engage in battle.

Just war theory is not applicable to total nuclear war, and that fact has led many Evangelical Christians to become nuclear pacifists.

PACIFISM

There are a growing number of Christians who believe that only total pacifism will enable us to neutralize the power of our enemies with love. Such Christians, aligning with the Anabaptist tradition, believe that if we live according to the Sermon on the Mount, we endeavor to overcome evil with good. Among their favorite verses are Romans 12:20-21:

> If your enemy is hungry, feed him; if he is thirsty, give him something to drink. In doing this, you will heap burning coals on his head. Do not be overcome by evil, but overcome evil with good.

Christians in the so-called "peace churches" ask if a better solution to the problems posed by Saddam Hussein would have been to make these verses national policy, rather than invading Iraq and bringing death and destruction into the lives of so many people.

According to the American Red Cross, half a million children under the age of 12 died as a direct result of the U.S. sanctions on Iraq.[5] There was supposed to be an arrangement by which, in exchange for oil, the basic needs of the Iraqi people were to be met, but thanks to the evil manipulations of Saddam Hussein, the help those children desperately needed never got to them. What if, those in peace churches contend, Christians had ignored the sanctions, bought medicine and food, took the supplies to Jordan and shipped them across the desert to meet the needs of desperate Iraqis? When you consider the billions of dollars churches have tied up in endowments and in buildings, it's clear that we could have saved hundreds of thousands of children from death. If we had, might Muslims across the Arab world be more open to the gospel? Would Christians now being persecuted in Iraq be spared?

Some Christians who support militarism contend that the ethical principles of Jesus are only applicable to individuals and were never meant to be applied on the societal level. Those in peace churches disagree; they say that if Christians had done what the Bible calls us to do for our enemies, we would have "heaped coals of fire" on Saddam Hussein's head. They contend that evil can be overcome with good, and that sacrificial love and the authority it generates will always triumph over power.

Mahatma Gandhi once suggested that everybody knows what Jesus taught—except for Christians. As a matter of fact, Gandhi claimed that he learned his principles of non-violent resistance to tyranny from the teachings of Christ.

When I consider the life of Gandhi and realize that he endeavored to live out the Sermon on the Mount more so than almost all the Christians I know, I am shaken. His efforts to deliver India from British rule and oppression adhered faithfully to the teachings of Jesus. Gandhi did not seek political revenge. Following the words of Christ, when he was hit on one cheek he turned the other. Yet he was by no means passive. He aggressively sought to love and disarm his enemies with his willingness to endure the worst punishment they could perpetrate. His capacity to love his enemies while submitting to their persecution makes him a strong example of what it means to imitate the lifestyle of Christ.

Gandhi studied the New Testament with zeal and could quote from the Scriptures in a way that would put most Bible school students to shame. He once entertained the possibility of becoming a Christian, but there were several circumstances that turned him away from this decision:

He had often seen the disparity between Christ and Christians. He said, "Stoning prophets and erecting churches to their memory afterwards has been the way of the world through the ages. Today we worship Christ, but the Christ in the flesh we crucified."

Gandhi lived in South Africa during the most formative period of his life, and a few nasty incidents there did little to disabuse him of his notions of Christianity. He encountered blatant discrimination in that ostensibly Christian society, being thrown off trains, excluded from hotels and restaurants, and made to feel unwelcome even in some Christian gatherings.

Gandhi graciously omits from his autobiography one more painful experience that occurred in South Africa. The Indian community especially admired a Christian named C.F. Andrews whom they themselves nicknamed "Christ's Faithful Apostle." Having heard so much about Andrews, Gandhi sought to hear him. But when C.F. Andrews was invited to speak in a church in South Africa, Gandhi was barred from the meeting—his skin color was not white.

Commenting on Gandhi's experiences in South Africa, E. Stanley Jones concludes, "Racialism has many sins to bear, but perhaps its worst sin was the obscuring of Christ in an hour when one of the greatest souls born of woman was making his decision."[6]

Gandhi came to believe that Christianity in its ecclesiastical form did not express the message of Jesus as set forth in the Sermon on the Mount. He saw that the Church, unlike Jesus, legitimized violence in the cause of justice and approved of war if doing so would protect its right to preach the gospel. Who knows what impact Christianity might have had on India if the father of that nation's independence had embraced our faith? Can it be that a Hindu understood the teachings of Jesus on love and power better than the theologians and preachers of Christ's Church? We will have to wait until Judgment Day for the answer.

CONNECTING VIOLENCE
WITH MATERIALISM

There is a connection between materialistic values and the promotion of militarism: Those of us who have possessions are anxious to protect what we have, regardless of the cost. We read these words in James 4:1-2:

> What causes fights and quarrels among you? Don't they come from your desires that battle within you? You want something but don't get it. You kill and covet, but you cannot have what you want. You quarrel and fight. You do not have, because you do not ask God.

Our failure to abandon power and live out love is often tied up with our materialistic lifestyles. We are so anxious to protect our possessions that we are willing to use all forms of force to ward off our enemies.

A few years ago at a conference of Mennonites, there was a discussion as to whether or not the pacifist position was still viable for their denomination. One elderly gentleman, who owned a huge farm and had great wealth, was very much in favor of abandoning the Mennonites' historical position in order to recognize circumstances when Christians could engage in war.

Challenging the wealthy gentleman was a younger man, who spoke passionately in defense of pacifism. When he had finished, the older man said, "It's all right for you to talk in this lofty manner, but one of these days they may come and take everything you have."

The young man responded, "This poses no problem for me. You see, sir, when I became a Christian I gave everything I had to Jesus. If they come, they can only take from me what belongs to Him, and that is His problem."

The older man retorted, "All right, so they can't take what you have because you have already given it to Jesus, but they can kill you."

The young man answered, "No, they can't. You see, sir, I am already dead. When I became a Christian, the life that belongs to this world came to an end, and the new life that I received in Christ can never be snuffed out."

In frustration the older man said, "They may not be able to take what you have and they may not be able to kill you, but let me tell you that they can make you suffer."

Once again the young man answered, "If that day comes, sir, I hope I will remember the words of Jesus, who said, 'Blessed are they who are persecuted for righteousness' sake; for theirs in the kingdom of heaven.' There is not much you can do to somebody who doesn't have anything, who is already dead and who rejoices in persecution."

That young man knew the secret that made the Early Church such a threat to the society of its day. People who have such an attitude toward property and life are free from societal control. They can afford the luxury of living dangerously and with total abandon to the will of God.

Perhaps the attitude of that young man has come of age. Perhaps the hour is at hand for more and more Christians to live out the Sermon on the Mount: turning from power as a means of resolving international conflicts and committing to sacrificial love instead. Will there arise a people who dare to make the loving of one's enemies a political philosophy? I myself am not there yet; but the more I consider it, the more I am aware that there may be no other option.

Several years ago, as a faculty member at the University of Pennsylvania, I was lecturing on the benefits of capitalism. A young man stood and voiced his opposition in very strong terms. I was startled. No one had ever opposed me so vehemently in all my years in the classroom.

I told the young man that he ought to sit down, lest I penalize him for his unruly behavior. He shouted back, "Who cares?"

Trying to restore order, I said, "Young man, you better behave yourself or I am going to put you out of this class."

To this he yelled, "Who cares?"

I then threatened that if he kept on in this belligerent manner, he probably wouldn't graduate from the university.

Again he yelled, "Who cares?"

It was obvious how the exchange would have gone on if I hadn't stopped. If I had told him that without a university education he would not be able to get a good job, he would again have answered, "Who cares?" And if I had gone on to explain that without a good job he wouldn't be able to buy all the material things that society says we have to have, he would have again yelled, "Who cares?"

As I have thought about that encounter over the years, my admiration for that young man's passion—misguided though it may have been—has grown. I have begun to suspect that it is only when Christians reach the point where we are able to yell, "Who cares?" to the empty allure of materialism that we will be able to follow Christ without reservation.

The Scripture tells us not to love the things of the world, because if we do, we expose ourselves as not having the Father's love within us (see 1 John 2:15). When things are our first priority, we inevitably resort to power to protect what we have against the encroachment of others. Only those who are free from material things are free to live out sacrificial love.

THE SINS OF THE POWERLESS

The way our discussion has progressed, one might be led to believe that sinfulness is a condition dangerous only for the powerful. Nothing could be further from the truth. In reality, the powerless are quite capable of being sinful. One sin to which they are especially prone is resentfulness. Often, the powerless are forced to accept conditions they detest that have been put in place by people in power over them, and they burn with resentment. They feel they have no way of striking back at those who oppress them, so they seethe with bitterness. When the powerless feel that they are the victims of forces beyond their control, they may say to themselves, *It's just not fair, but there's nothing I can do about it*. Such feelings are dangerous.

Resentment was at the root of the terrorist attacks on September 11, 2001. The Egyptians and Saudis who flew the airplanes into the World Trade Center and the Pentagon on 9/11 were not poor and uneducated men. Almost all of them were university graduates who were part of the upper-middle class establishment of their respective societies. However, they shared a deep resentment of the West and of the United States in particular. Their bitterness sprang from a general perception that their ancient culture was being undermined by encroaching oppression from the West, and they focused their resentments on the specific situation between Israel and the Palestinians. They felt powerless to stop Israelis from driving Palestinians from the land that was ceded to the Israelis when the United Nations created the state of Israel. At that time, territory was designated to provide for a free and autonomous Palestinian state—a state that has never yet been established. For decades, Muslims the world over have watched the Palestinians suffer, and their resentment has grown. Resentment is the root out of which grows bitterness (see Heb. 12:15), and out of bitterness comes destruction. Bitterness led 19 men to murder nearly 3,000 innocent victims on September 11.

The word "resentment" comes from two Latin roots: *re* and *sentire*. *Sentire* means "to feel" and *re* means "again." Thus, to resent means *to feel over and over again* the anger, bitterness and hatred that well up in reaction to injustices endured at the hands of the powerful.

GENDER RESENTMENTS

I know wives who resent their husbands. They feel trapped in their roles as homemakers, and they feel taken for granted and used. These women feel reduced to servile creatures whose only responsibility is to cater to the wishes of their husbands. They resent that they work hard all day and yet are often presumed to have been relaxing and taking it easy. They resent it when their husbands say, "You don't know what it's like to go out and work for a living."

They feel like replying, "You don't know what it's like to stay home and mind children, wash diapers, do laundry, scrub showers and bathtubs, pick up after you and the children, and run a taxi service for everybody in this family."

Today, many women are employed outside the home. Yet studies show that when a woman has a job, her responsibilities for the needs of the household are not usually diminished. In many cases, even when the wife works, the husband does not pitch in with housework and child-rearing, nor do the children step up to help. Instead, the working wife and mother finds that she is expected to do all she did before she was employed, in spite of the fact that she now puts in an eight-hour work-day. Such a woman resents it when her husband comes home, throws himself on the sofa, and shouts toward the kitchen, "I've had a tough day. When will dinner be ready?" She further resents it when her children say, "The clothes I want to wear tomorrow aren't washed." That her husband and children do not share the responsibility of maintaining the household leaves her feeling angry, hurt and resentful.

The feminist movement has taught us all some important lessons. Raising children, keeping house and doing other family chores should be shared responsibilities. Expecting women to take care of stereotypical "women's work" in addition to working outside the home is unreasonable in the extreme. Sharing in the responsibilities that go with maintaining a family and a home is essential to allay the resentments that young mothers and wives are prone to experience at the mercy of our culture's gender-biased expectations. Such resentments can lead to family conflicts and even divorce.

I am becoming increasingly sensitive to the values proposed by many feminists. Their angry rhetoric we saw especially in the 1960s and 1970s arose, I believe, out of resentment that had been building among women for centuries. Generations of women have endured oppression of all kinds at the hands of sexist men, suffering indignity, marginalization and sexual exploitation. Many feminists during the heyday of the women's movement couldn't say "No more!" loudly enough.

Years ago, my son and I were in New York City on a Saturday afternoon. We walked by a movie theater marquee on Times Square that announced a showing of *Snuff*, a pornographic movie that included everything vile about the ways men have treated women. This particular film had an exceptionally debased climax: a naked woman was stabbed to death. It was rumored at the time that the stabbing, rather than being staged, was in fact real—that the woman's sadistic rape and murder actually took place and was captured "live" for the movie. The advertisement on the billboard read, "Made in Argentina, Where Life Is Cheap."

On that Saturday afternoon, a group of more than 50 feminists had gathered outside the movie theater and were marching in a circle to protest the film. In addition to carrying placards that made clear their disgust with and opposition to the movie, the women were chanting, "Life is never cheap! Life is never cheap! Life is never cheap!"

My son and I stood and watched the demonstration for several minutes, and then I said to him, "We should join them; we should be a part of this demonstration. The Church of Jesus Christ should be here voicing its condemnation. Opposition to this film should not be left solely to the feminist movement." My son agreed and we joined in the picketing.

After we marched for two or three minutes, one of the leaders of the protest came up to us and asked, "What are you doing here? There is no place for men in this protest. Don't you understand? You are the enemy! We despise you!"

I responded gently, "We are marching anyway; you do not own the exclusive right to be angry with evil." On the one hand, I was taken aback by her meanness. On the other hand, I sympathized with her reaction. She was experiencing resentment. She was voicing her reaction to pain inflicted by male oppression and articulating the anger of women who have been victimized by a sexist society that regularly teaches men to view women's bodies solely as objects of pleasure. She was reacting to a culture that has given men permission to gain sexual excitement from exercising power over and even inflicting suffering on women.

It is not enough for Christians to sympathize with the complaints of feminists; we must recognize the rightness and truth in much of what they say to us. Martin Buber, the Jewish philosopher, differentiated between "I-It" relationships and "I-Thou" relationships.[1] In an I-It relationship, the other person is treated as an object or a thing that can be used to serve one's interests and desires with little regard for the other person. On the other hand, an I-Thou relationship recognizes a sacredness in the other person.

An I-Thou relationship at its best is a very spiritual thing. A spirit-filled person will not simply look *at* the other, but will look *into* the other. Empowered by the Holy Spirit, it is possible to look into another's eyes, reach down into the depths of that person's being and connect with the essential self of the other.

Some Christians interpret Matthew 6:22-23 as Jesus' way of saying that it is through our eyes that we can break through the barriers of darkness that keep us from connecting with others in the intimate way Christ intends. There is a hunger among church people for a deeper understanding of what it means to love and how love is facilitated by the Holy Spirit. Church leaders have been so preoccupied with what is and is not acceptable erotic behavior that they have given scant attention to understanding the ways and means for creating love. Young people are raised on the dos and the don'ts of sexual behavior, but given very little instruction on relating with another in such a way that the other person becomes a sacred "thou," rather than a usable "it." If we could learn from Jesus and be enabled by the Holy Spirit to look *into* one another and connect with each other's sacredness, I believe that sexual exploitation would end.

Even as we acknowledge the resentments common to modern women, we should also recognize that there are husbands who resent their wives for various reasons. It may be because their wives are so much more adept at social gatherings than they. Sociological studies indicate that women tend to have better verbal skills than men and they find it much easier to talk to strangers and to function in social situations.[2] When they go out with their husbands, such women may be the life of the party while their husbands stand in the background, grumbling and feeling deep resentment.

Another source of resentment increasingly common among men comes from being accused of male chauvinism and domination, often without just cause. Radical feminists, particularly in the 1960s and 1970s, had an unfortunate tendency to paint all men with the same brush. Such indiscriminate accusations label many decent, hardworking men as evil perpetrators of female oppression—when this is just not the case. There are many men who feel unfairly under attack, and they are not only confused, but also have boiling resentments bottled up inside. They see themselves condemned for doing what they believed they signed up to do when they got married.

There is a good, biblical basis for changing the roles traditionally prescribed for men, but change must not be coerced. Men, like other human beings, are much more likely to have a change of heart under the influence of sacrificial love, rather than coercive power.

RESENTFUL PARENTS AND CHILDREN

I know mothers who resent their children. They seldom verbalize this resentment, but it is there nevertheless. Some prepared themselves for personally rewarding careers and then suddenly found that they were pregnant. Babies born to such women interfere (albeit unintentionally) with carefully laid plans and dreams. Some mothers-to-be pretend that they are thrilled with their pregnancies, never letting on that they are suffering from inner bitterness. They never verbalize their resentment, but it is there.

Otto Pollak, a friend of mine and one of the most brilliant scholars in the field of family studies, found that a mother's repressed resentment is felt and known by the children.[3] He suggested that children are experts at picking up nonverbal communication. While their mothers say all the right things and make all the proper gestures of love and affection, the children sense repressed resentments. Much of the maladjustment among young people in today's society, Pollak contended, is the result of being reared by mothers who resent them.

Nothing in the socialization of modern women prepares them for motherhood. They are educated in the same schools as men and given the same professional options. They are inspired by the same possibilities and taught to expect vocational successes that in previous generations were reserved for men. I believe that this is exactly the way it should be, for I am firmly convinced that women should be allowed to realize their potential and exercise their gifts. However, it should be obvious that for many women, having children is an interruption of the lives they had planned. On the surface, such mothers may gallantly accept the disruptions of their plans, but inwardly they resent the intrusion; they have been forced into a role they are unable to reject. Feeling trapped and cheated out of the "good life" they envisioned for themselves, resentment flares in their hearts and minds. This resentment is sin.

In our society, there are many parents whose resentments seem justified in light of their children's behavior. I know parents who have made fantastic sacrifices to provide the best of everything for their children. They have made sure that their children had the best clothing, the best education possible, every form of recreation and entertainment and all the emotional support they could give. Such provisions were made with great sacrifice, yet, in far too many cases, the children have treated what they have received as rights rather than privileges. They do not act as though their parents have done anything special for them. They go off to college, career or marriage and live their lives with almost total indifference to their parents' desire to see or hear from them. It would take so little effort to telephone now and then, to send a letter or plan a visit home. But these children care little about the parents who did so much for them.

The parents are powerless to change the situation—they can't *make* their children care. They say to themselves, *It doesn't seem fair, after all we did for them,* and they are understandably resentful. But resentment, regardless of how justified it may appear to be, is really sin.

I know children, on the other hand, who resent their parents. One woman had a father who beat her and sexually molested her as a child. She was powerless to stop him from putting her through these painful ordeals. When she told her mother what was going on, her mom refused to believe her and punished her for lying. Until this day, resentment burns within that daughter. Day by day, she "re-feels" the anger and hatred of her youth.

So many people resent their parents for not loving them as they felt they deserved. I wonder how many people would say, "My parents always loved my brother more than they loved me, and I resent them for that." Having no power to force their parents to give them the love they desperately crave, such children allow themselves to feel over and over again the hurt and rejection they experienced—this is the sin of resentment.

Oppressed people, whether women, men, parents or children, are all prone to resentment. Whenever the powerless have to endure indignities and pain at the hands of those who have power, they feel justified in their hatred and anger. But what they feel is justified is actually sin in the eyes of God.

Churches have done very little to help people and families deal with these resentments. "Family life" conferences I have attended have usually reinforced traditional, and sometimes unbiblical, roles for husbands and wives. These roles made great sense in a pre-industrial, agrarian society, but have become increasingly dysfunctional in our modern world. Using certain carefully selected verses to legitimize their arguments, the leaders of these conferences have reinforced the value of submission to oppression, rather than spelling out how family members can live in freedom together through sacrificial love, seeking to serve each other in the name of Christ.

RACIAL RESENTMENT

African-American people often resent white people. When they do not, it is primarily because they have, through the grace of God, developed a very special capacity to forgive those whom they have every reason to resent. For hundreds of years, relationships between American blacks and whites have exposed myriad abuses of power. White people ripped Africans from their homeland and brought them in chains across the sea to be enslaved and humiliated. After more than four centuries, black slaves were emancipated—but they were still kept in a state of powerlessness. Refusing to regard those who had previously been their slaves, whites constructed a system of discrimination and oppression designed to diminish the dignity of African-Americans and crush their spirits for yet another century. Still today, nearly five decades after the Civil Rights Act, there are systemic injustices that disproportionately affect the African-American community. These injustices may not be deliberate, but they are real.

One cannot work within the African-American community without being sensitive to this long-running resentment and feeling it on every side. Yet in spite of the rational justification for such a reaction, resentment is still a sin. Christians of every color must repent of it by the grace of God.

John Perkins is a good friend of mine and one of the great Christians of our time. This outstanding black leader has spearheaded life-changing social and economic development programs for African-Americans in the state of Mississippi, and has inspired many similar projects in other parts of the nation and around the world. John understands the indignities his brothers and sisters suffer as a result of racism. He knows the humiliation his people endure in a society that, in spite of its democratic rhetoric, has treated African-American men and women as an inferior caste. He knows because he has experienced it firsthand. He explains:

I was about eleven years old when I got a powerful lesson in economics. It was a lesson which helped me see why poor families like mine stayed poor while the rich got richer.

I stood on a farmer's back porch, waiting for him to come back with the money. I was bone tired; that good kind of tired that comes after a hard day's work. The kind of tired a boy earns doing a man's worth of hauling on a hot, humid summer day in Mississippi.

But if my body was remembering the day's work, my mind was flying ahead to what I could do with the dollar or dollar-and-a-half that would soon be in my pocket. Would I buy a shiny new pocket knife? That would really wow the guys back home. Or what about a wallet?

Not that I really needed these things, you see. But I was a few miles away from home. For kids in our town that was big stuff. Vacations were always an occasion for bragging—so much so that the kids who did not go on vacations had to invent them.

So that's how this thing got started, this custom of buying something while you were gone to prove where you had been. What you bought wasn't all that important. What mattered was what it would prove.

The farmer came through the kitchen onto the back porch. I held out my hand expectantly. Into it fell—I could hardly believe it—just two coins! A dime and a buffalo nickel! I stared into my hand. If that farmer had knocked the wind out of me, I couldn't have been any more surprised. Or hurt. Or humiliated.

I had been used. And I couldn't do a single thing about it. Everything in me wanted to throw that blasted money on the floor and stomp out of there.

But I couldn't. I knew what white people said about smart niggers. I knew better than to be one of those.

I shuffled off that back porch, head down, ashamed, degraded, violated. I didn't want anyone to know I had been exploited. I hated myself.[4]

However, John has been touched by the Holy Spirit. He has overcome his resentment and loves those whom the world would say he has every right to hate. He knows that the Bible leaves no room for resentment; and through the power of the Holy Spirit, John Perkins has found a way to love those who deceitfully used him. Jesus said, "I tell you: Love your enemies and pray for those who persecute you" (Matt. 5:44), and with God's help, John is doing just that.

RESENTING GOD

There is one form of resentment that some Christians seldom, if ever, admit: the resentment they feel toward God. They view themselves as powerless, see God as powerful and resent that God has not used that power on their behalf.

One young woman was engaged to be married to someone who was not a Christian. Her pastor advised her not to go through with the wedding because, as he interpreted Scripture, the Bible clearly teaches that Christians are not supposed to marry non-Christians. He read to her, "Do not be yoked together with unbelievers. For what do righteousness and wickedness have in common? Or what fellowship can light have with darkness?" (2 Cor. 6:14). Her pastor said that she should break off the relationship and trust the Lord to bring a Christian man into her life. He assured her that God had somebody else in store for her future. The young woman did as she was told and as she believed the Bible taught—but no Christian man came into her life.

This woman is now in her late 30s and there is a bitterness within her. She feels betrayed by God and believes that God cannot be trusted. She never says so out loud, but you can sense it in the way she lives, acts and talks. She resents God deeply. I can imagine her saying, *It just isn't fair, God. You have given other women husbands. Women less attractive than I am are married. There are people who love You less and are less committed to You than I am, and they have husbands. Here I am alone, forsaken, and I will probably die that way. It just isn't fair!*

I know a couple who are attractive, intelligent and prosperous. They have a lovely home and good educational backgrounds. Most important, they have the ways and means to take care of a child. They have prayed and pleaded with the Lord to give them a child, but none has come. I can imagine what they think as they look at teenage single women living in poverty with more children than they know how to handle. I imagine them saying, "It just isn't fair. To women who don't even want babies, You give children that they will never love or care for, and yet You have denied us a baby. We would have made such good parents. We would have been so faithful in our responsibilities to raise a child in the ways of Scripture. It just isn't fair!" From a rational perspective, that couple has every reason to be resentful. But this resentment must be dealt with, lest it destroy them both.

While still in graduate school, I served a small church on weekends. In that church, there was a man who had once been a faithful attendee. He gave up on the Church and on Christianity when he watched his eight-year-old son die a painful death in the grip of incurable leukemia.

One day, while visiting this bitter man, I tried to tell him that he shouldn't give up on God because of what had happened. I explained that

I could understand why he had turned away and no longer believed that there was a God, given what he had watched his dear boy go through during the days of his sickness. I'll never forget his response: "You don't get it, do you, Tony? I still believe in God. There is no doubt in my mind that there is a God. I don't go to church anymore because I hate God!"

I knew that there were no explanations or arguments I could offer to dissuade him, but I believe there is a God who embraces that man and is trying to get him to listen to a soft, still voice that says, "I understand." I trust that God can show extra grace to a dear brother who has had to endure such pain.

A friend of mine tells a story about a similarly despairing man who was consumed by grief after the death of his son. The man went to see his pastor and asked, "Where was God when my son died?"

The compassionate pastor gently answered, "The same place He was when His Son died."

In the end, it may be that all we can offer those who have experienced disappointment in God is an assurance that God understands pain and suffering firsthand. A God who empathizes in our times of sorrow is a God who can help us grow past our resentments into sacrificial love.

There are pastors who are filled with resentment. They have labored hard and long in their communities. They have prayed, visited, preached, counseled. They have put endless hours into administration and sacrificed themselves and their families for the welfare and growth of their churches—but all to no avail. Their churches have not grown, the spiritual results of their efforts seem meager and their accomplishments seem ineffective. These pastors look around and see other clergy who seem less committed, less orthodox, less prayerful and more worldly, but whose churches flourish and grow. Those other pastors are revered and honored, and their success plants the seed of resentment in clergy who feel like failures. They feel that God has not been fair with them. They may not say it. They may repress it behind an air of piety, but resentment eats away within them as over and over again they feel anger toward the Almighty.

In the suburban community where my school, Eastern University, is located, a new church plant began attracting large numbers of people to its worship services. It was an Evangelical church, and the energy and spontaneity of its worship proved to be a magnet that drew people away from the older, established mainline churches in the neighborhood. The pastor of one of those churches said to me, "Every time I drive by that place, I wish I had a bomb to throw at their building." He eventually left the community, moving to another part of the country, because he could not deal with his resentment. Spirituality, in its finest form, enables us to be more than conquerors over such resentments.

When my son was in high school, he went out for the soccer team in a school where soccer was a big-time sport. To his surprise, he became the starting goalie during his freshman year and helped the team all the way to the state championship game. The downside was that he bumped a senior from the starting line-up. The older player had every expectation of being the goalie until my son Bart came along. But instead of wallowing in resentment, the young man rode the bench without a word of complaint. He played not a single game his entire senior year, but was a constant and enthusiastic cheerleader for Bart. What's more, he regularly offered to pick Bart up and drive him to games and practices.

One Saturday morning, my son got up very early. I looked out our bedroom window and saw him running to his friend's car. Bart didn't return until three hours later. When he came into the house, he told me that it had been a very special morning. His friend, the player Bart had displaced as goalie, had led him to make a commitment of his life to Christ. Bart gave his life over to Jesus and promised to serve Christ for the rest of his life.

His friend's resentment was overcome by the grace of God. What could have been a source of bitterness was turned into joy. From that day on, the young man who had been bumped out of the goalie box could look at my son and the ministries Bart developed in the years that followed and see them as the direct results of his own God-given ability to overcome resentment.

CONFESSION AND PRAYER

The first thing the powerless must do, as they writhe under the sin and agony of their resentments, is to confess before God that what they are feeling is wrong. They must stop justifying themselves and recognize that the Bible does not leave room for resentment. They should remember what Scripture says:

> You, my brothers, were called to be free. But do not use your freedom to indulge the sinful nature; rather, serve one another in love. The entire law is summed up in a single command: "Love your neighbor as yourself." If you keep on biting and devouring each other, watch out or you will be destroyed by each other (Gal. 5:13-15).

Jesus wants to deliver us from the backbiting, bitterness and pain of resentment. He wants to set us free from these destructive emotions because resentment keeps us from enjoying life and from appreciating the blessings He planned for us. People who suffer from resentment lose the ability to appreciate the many beautiful things God has provided for their enjoyment.

The beginning of freedom from resentment is confession. Thus, it is crucial for the powerless who suffer from resentment to confess that their justifications for resentment are not pleasing to God—that is, they are sin. Confession is a prerequisite to being cleansed from sin. The Scriptures read, "If we confess our sins, he is faithful and just and will forgive us our sins and purify us from all unrighteousness. If we claim we have not sinned, we make him out to be a liar and his word has no place in our lives" (1 John 1:9-10).

Once we have confessed, repented and been forgiven through God's infinite grace, we may still have to work to kill the seeds of resentment, lest they return. Church tradition holds that resentment can be eradicated from the consciousness of Christians by surrendering to the mystical, transformative power of God through prayer. I teach my students what St. Ignatius called "centering prayer." It is a process whereby the Christian focuses in silence on Christ, driving all else out of his heart and mind, until Christ alone is the preoccupation of prayer. (There is an old gospel song that tells us to turn our eyes upon Jesus and look full in His wonderful face, and the things of earth will grow strangely dim.) That, in a sense, is what I am talking about. It takes me about 10 minutes to become inwardly still and, in that quietude, to wait for the Holy Spirit to permeate my being. In such a state of quiet surrender to Christ, the resentful feelings eating away within me are cleansed from my consciousness little by little, and I come gradually to enjoy a lightness of heart and an unburdened soul.

There are certain things, as Jesus said, that can only be accomplished "through prayer and fasting" (see Mark 9:14-29), and having considered the intractability of resentment, I am convinced that it takes a miracle of the Spirit to deliver me from its clutches. Resentment can only come out through prayer.

When Jesus hung on the cross, He transcended our time-space continuum; in His divinity, He was (and is) able to apprehend every single moment in time simultaneously. When He said, "Before Abraham was,

I am!" He wasn't using poor grammar; He was saying that thousands of years earlier, before Abraham was even born, was a time that *was* present tense for Him, right then and there. In His humanity, Jesus experienced time as we do: Events occurred in consecutive fashion, within a linear progression toward the future. But Jesus was also God, and in His divinity He was able to be the Alpha and Omega, the Beginning and the End. He was able to gather into Himself all moments of time in what some theologians, such as Emil Brunner, have called the "eternal now." With Jesus, because He is God, a thousand years are as a day and a day as a thousand years (see 2 Pet. 3:8).[5]

I say all this because I believe that, as He hung on the cross, Jesus, the One who never sinned, was (and is) simultaneously with every sinner in every moment of that person's life. On Calvary's tree, He was and is simultaneously with you and with me in our sin, and will, as Scripture suggests, absorb into Himself the resentments we harbor. Isaiah 53:5 says that through His sufferings we are healed. As we confess our sins, I believe that Jesus reaches across time and space and takes hold of them, absorbing them into Himself. He reaches out from Calvary to all who are open to Him, draining away resentment and replacing it with love.

But as it says in 1 John 1:9, it all begins with confession.

I can suggest no neat socio-psychological technique developed through social science research that provides deliverance from resentment. None exists. There is only one way to get rid of resentment: to confess it and ask Jesus to cleanse you from it. I believe that when you make this request, passionately and sincerely, the resurrected Jesus spiritually enters into your soul and removes these feelings from which you cannot rid yourself. You might want to pray this prayer:

Lord, You know these feelings I have. You know how they are destroying me and keeping me from enjoying life. You know that I have tried to repress them and forget them, but it hasn't worked. Lord, I can't remove the resentments, so I ask You to do it. Please enter my life and purge me from this bitterness. Amen.

BECOMING A FORGIVER

The final thing we must do is ask God to enable us to forgive the person against whom we harbor resentments. A sheer determination of the will is not adequate. What is needed is a gift of love from God. God's love, flowing into us as we yield to God in prayer, can make us into forgiving people. This is something that takes place within the individual. Through an ongoing yieldedness to the work of the Holy Spirit, the grace of God manifests itself in grace to those toward whom we have had resentment.

Those who have resentments against God must prayerfully say to Him, "God, I forgive You." That may sound blasphemous at first blush, an assumption that God has done something wrong. On a logical level, we all know that God has not done any such thing. Resentments toward God are unjustified, built on the falsehood that the hurts and tragedies in our lives are God's doing or God's will. This ignores the fact that Satan, and those who serve with him, constantly bring suffering and death into our lives and raise havoc in our world. There is no simple answer as to why so many painful and ugly things are allowed to happen in God's world, but I must stress that when Jesus was tempted by Satan, as recorded in Luke 4, Christ did not challenge the claim that Satan exercises great power over "the kingdoms of the world." What further evidence do we need, other than reading the headlines of today's newspapers, that the evil one is responsible for much that happens on this planet, even as we live in anticipation of the day when Christ returns and the kingdoms of this world become the kingdom of our God? There are evil forces at work that add to the sufferings that are part and parcel of human existence.

While we may *know* intellectually that we have not been wronged by God, many of us *feel* differently. This being the case, it's entirely warranted to pray from the heart, rather than the head:

God, I feel that You have wronged me. I forgive You. Someday when You explain all of this to me, I will see that it was ridiculous to even pray this prayer. But between now and then, I want to end these feelings of hostility toward You. Forgive me for feeling like I have to forgive You. In Jesus' name. Amen.

Many years ago, when Jack Paar was the host of *The Tonight Show*, his music director was a pianist named José Melis. Occasionally on the show, something remarkable happened: Jack Paar would go over to the piano and, in an indiscriminate way, come down on the piano keys, striking a discord. He would then say to José Melis, "Okay, José, let's see what you can do with that."

José would put his fingers on the exact keys that Paar had struck and then blend those clashing notes into a beautiful, harmonious piece of music. He turned the discord into a melody.

As we grow in the Spirit, we will increasingly trust God to take the painful discords struck in our lives and blend them into something beautiful and good. Not all things are good when they happen, but a proper understanding of Romans 8:28 leads us to trust that God can use the most painful evil to produce good in our lives. If we give over our resentment, God will replace it with love.

THE PAINFUL COST OF CONQUERING LOVE

When it comes to power, nobody has more than God. The heavens declare God's glory. All of nature gives evidence of what God can do. God's word can command anything to come out of nothing. God holds all things together.

Knowledge about the power of God leads inevitably to questions about why God does not use this power as we feel God should. There are wars God should stop, yet God allows them to grind on to their destructive conclusions. God should heal the sick and make the blind see, yet in most cases modern medicine can be credited with any healing that takes place. God should be able to keep tragedies from happening, yet they happen. God should feed all the hungry of the world, yet many starve.

If God is so powerful, why doesn't God make this the best of all possible worlds? Why doesn't God set things right? Why doesn't God abolish evil? It is not enough to say that it is not God's will that all evils be corrected on the final day of the Lord, or that there are great lessons God can teach us through such trials, or that terrible events are part of some wonderful plan that we will one day understand. When the victims of tragedy, injustice and absurd events ask "Why?" these worn-out answers do not suffice.

Too often, we Christians try to make excuses for God so that the Almighty won't look so bad to those who have suffered "the slings and arrows of outrageous fortune"—as Shakespeare expressed it. We make a case for the *goodness* of God to those who want to know how a *loving* God can allow so many bad things to happen to so many good people.

In endeavoring to bring words of comfort to suffering people like the man in my congregation who lost his son to leukemia, well-meaning people sometimes say that such tragedies are all part of God's plan and that one day, some day, we will see what God had in mind when God allowed or even caused such painful and tragic events. While the intention may be to comfort, such words can turn those who suffer away from God.

A friend of mine lost his handsome young son when he fell to his death while attempting to climb a mountain. At the funeral, the minister who was leading the service declared, "We must all accept this tragedy as part of God's plan and accept it as God's will here on earth."

My friend stood and shouted, "This was *not* God's will! When my son died, God was the first one who cried!"

We cannot attribute the ugly, evil and tragic things that go on in this world to God. God is not the author of evil. There is an evil power at work in the world, and while Evangelicals acknowledge the existence of Satan, they seldom attribute any of life's tragedies to the prince of darkness.

Furthermore, I believe that Romans 8:28 might be better translated like this: *In the midst of everything that is happening, God is at work in us and through us, and eventually can bring some good out of what is presently tragic.*

Yet these answers do not answer *the* question: Why doesn't an all-powerful God intercede and prevent the sufferings and tragedies that cause us so much pain?

In 1981, a Jewish rabbi, Harold Kushner, wrote a bestseller titled *When Bad Things Happen to Good People.*[1] Rabbi Kushner's son was the victim of a disease that caused rapid aging, and he watched helplessly as his dear boy grew old and died before the age of 12. As a religious leader, he knew all the "right" answers. He knew that he was supposed to say that this tragedy was part of some great plan and that through the suffering, wonderful blessings would come. He knew that he was supposed to believe that through this trial, God was teaching him and helping him grow. He knew all the pat answers to suffering taught in theological seminaries; he had read the books and had heard all the arguments—but none of them worked. All of them rang hollow. None of the old answers brought him comfort.

After much thought, Rabbi Kushner concluded that God wanted to help but His power was limited. Kushner came to believe that God loved his boy but did not have the power to stop all the suffering in the world. Strangely, this answer did not upset him. Quite the opposite. He came to feel good about God, and concluded that it was better to have a God who cared but could not always help than to have a God who could help but did not care. Rabbi Kushner concluded that God was all-loving but not all-powerful.

In personal conversations with Rabbi Kushner, he made it clear to me that *omnipotence* is not a word that appears in the Hebrew Bible. Omnipotence is a Greek concept. In the Hebrew Scriptures, God is described as *more powerful* than all the other gods—but that is far different than saying that God is omnipotent. One of the most famous of contemporary Jewish scholars and rabbis, Abraham Heschel, makes a similar claim: that omnipotence is a concept that emerged out of the Hellenistic world.[2] This concept stands in opposition to the Hebraic God, whose life is marked by pathos and who weeps for humanity, even as He endeavors to work through righteous people to alleviate the sufferings that mark this world.

Rabbi Kushner believes in a God who is at work in the world, endeavoring to transform creation into the kind of world described by the prophet Isaiah:

"Behold, I will create new heavens and a new earth. The former things will not be remembered, nor will they come to mind. But be glad and rejoice forever in what I will create, for I will create Jerusalem to be a delight and its people a joy. I will rejoice over Jerusalem and take delight in my people; the sound of weeping and of crying will be heard in it no more. Never again will there be in it an infant who lives but a few days, or an old man who does not live out his years; he who dies at a hundred will be thought a mere youth; he who fails to reach a hundred will be considered accursed. They will build houses and dwell in them; they will plant vineyards and eat their fruit. No longer will they build houses and others live in them, or plant and others eat. For as the days of a tree, so will be the days of my people; my chosen ones will long enjoy the works of their hands. They will not toil in vain or bear children doomed to misfortune; for they will be a people blessed by the LORD, they and their descendants with them. Before they call I will answer; while they are still speaking I will hear. The wolf and the lamb will feed together, and the lion will eat straw like the ox, but dust will be the serpent's food. They will neither harm nor destroy on all my holy mountain," says the LORD (Isa. 65:17-25).

In this struggle to create the world that ought to be, God calls on people like you and me to work for the justice and the wellbeing that is intended for all humanity. In the Hebrew Bible, the God of Israel is seen as being involved in the historical struggles of the human race, and calls for us to become co-laborers in these efforts.

A LIMITED GOD?

Perhaps there are some Christians who are uncomfortable with the idea that God is not able to stop all suffering. To them I want to wholeheartedly affirm that God *will* overcome all evil one day and that "Jesus shall reign where'er the sun does its successive journeys run."[3] Some-day, perhaps sooner than we think, Jesus will return to bring all things under His control. The Scriptures say, "For he must reign until he has put all his enemies under his feet. The last enemy to be destroyed is death" (1 Cor. 15:25-26).

However, between now and that hour, God's power *is* limited—but God's limitation is *self-imposed*. Rabbi Kushner agrees; according to Hebrew theology, he says, God had to withdraw from occupying all time and space in order to make room for our universe. God pulled back to allow for creation.

A limited God? A God who is not presently all-powerful? A God who here and now lacks omnipotence? Such ideas may boggle the mind and reek of heresy. Doesn't orthodox Christianity say that God can do anything but fail? We Evangelicals have hailed the Lord God as the One who controls all earthly events—yet it may be that our strong declarations of God's omnipotence fail to acknowledge that God may *deliberately* choose not to use His power, and does so out of love.

Stop to consider that in the Garden of Eden, God gave freedom to Adam and Eve, knowing that within that freedom was the possibility that the first couple in history could disobey His will. With freedom came the real possibility that His will would not always be done. If we stop to think about it, we have to acknowledge that if Adam and Eve and their children had the capacity to love God, then God gave them freedom to reject Him—and that's exactly what God did. Without freedom, there could be no love; and love, which is of ultimate importance to God, would not be a possibility for us. *God had to let go of power if we were to be free to love*, because love can never be coerced. It can never be forced. It must always be freely given.

Parents know this. Parents know that relinquishing power is a precondition to their children coming of age and expressing the kind of mature love and commitments that make them into the magnificent human beings God means for them to be.

Limiting power is a precondition for freedom and freedom is a precondition to love. In the end, it is love, especially in its sacrificial form, that marks every citizen who has freely chosen to be a part of the kingdom of God.

Science-fiction novelists imagine the future, sometimes describing a world that is problem-free. Aldous Huxley's *Brave New World* and George Orwell's *1984* explore futures in which people exchange their freedom for no more sorrow and suffering. These authors realized that in such a world, there could be no more love because love requires freedom. Understanding the doctrine of "original sin" better than most theologians, they knew that, given freedom, people choose to do things that bring sorrow and suffering and, in their visions of a world free of sorrow and suffering, there could be no freedom and, consequently, no love.

If God had come to us in power instead of as a baby in a manger, we would have had no choice: We would be as nothing before Him, groveling before His throne and trembling in His presence. But God comes to us in love and invites us to be His friends (see John 15:14-15), giving us a choice.

When all is said and done, I find comfort in the verse that tells me, "God is love" (1 John 4:8). Stop to think about it: If given the choice between living in a world governed by God's power or a world permeated by God's love, wouldn't you choose the latter? Only in a world permeated by God's love do you have freedom.

THE GOD WHO COMES IN WEAKNESS

In the birth of Jesus, God entered history as a vulnerable infant. On that first Christmas, YHWH was incarnated in a child. He would grow up like other children. He would have times when, like other children, He would be tired and need rest and sleep. He would have to study, ask questions and learn from His elders. To the other children of Nazareth, He probably seemed very much like them. He lived among them with all the weaknesses of a growing child, but with one difference: He was without sin. He resisted evil and lived a pure life not by depending on Himself, but, instead, it was in His dependence on the Father that Jesus found the wherewithal to conquer the temptations of His flesh. He was as human as any of us, but He grew in loving fellowship with His Father, and therein found strength to overcome the evil one.

When the early leaders of Christendom came together to designate which of the many books written about Jesus should be included in the canon (the accepted books that would eventually make up our Bible), they found it necessary to reject some writings that had gained popularity among Christians. In one of the rejected books, the child Jesus is described as playing with some of the boys of Nazareth. A few of them are mean to Jesus and treat Him with great cruelty. Jesus responds by raising His hand to these children and striking them dead. In another story, Jesus is playing in the mud with some of His friends. He and the others set themselves to the task of making models of animals out of the clay. Jesus makes some clay birds and finishes off His project by making His birds come to life and fly away.[4]

These writings were never included in Scripture for an obvious reason: The stories are totally out of character with the nature of Christ. God did not incarnate Himself as a superboy who would dazzle His peers with magic tricks. The Church Fathers knew that Jesus grew up as one of us, taking on our frailties and weaknesses. In Jesus, God had abandoned power and majesty in order to enter human history as One whom we could imitate. If it had been otherwise, God would not have been able to ask us to be like Him.

Not only did God give up power when He was incarnated in Jesus, but in the incarnation God also gave up omniscience.

A friend of mine who often speaks to students at Christian colleges regularly asks the question, "Did Jesus understand radar?" In many cases the students answer, "Yes!" They fail to recognize that if Jesus, living 2,000 years ago, had understood a twentieth-century invention, He would not have been a human being. The Incarnation would have been a "put-on." His humanity would have been a pretense. Such was not the case. He really was born as one of us. The ancient Chalcedonian Creed says with clarity that Jesus was "very man, of very man."

Such ideas about God are revolutionary to some and controversial to all. Yet putting God into a box defined by Greek philosophers rather than declaring the God who is revealed in the Bible as loving vulnerably is a serious mistake.

To sum up, I believe in a God who has self-imposed limitations on power in order to give us freedom to choose love and justice, even if such freedom carries with it the possibility that we might choose otherwise. I believe in a God who is at work in the world through people who freely choose to become instruments through which God's will can be done on earth as it is in heaven. I believe, as one theologian has proposed, in a *God who empowers* rather than *an all-powerful God*. Our God of love empowers us to love, to live out the Great Commandment to love God and our neighbor.

MODERN-DAY GNOSTICISM

It is disturbing to me that among the theologians of our day there are some who doubt the divinity of Christ. Many such unorthodox scholars refuse to believe that Jesus was the full and complete Incarnation of God.

It's fascinating that this contemporary heresy—doubting the divinity of Jesus—is exactly the opposite of the most common heresy expressed during the times of the Early Church: doubting the *humanity* of Jesus. The ancient heretics found it inconceivable and totally unbelievable that a pure and holy God should take on the physical nature of man, because prominent Greek philosophers had taught that the flesh was inherently evil. One group of heretics, called the Gnostics, claimed that Jesus only *appeared* to have a human body. In reality, they claimed, He was an omnipotent, spiritual presence pretending to be a man. So pervasive was this heresy among the early Christians that John had to make a special emphasis on Jesus' humanity when he wrote in his Gospel: "And the Word was made flesh, and dwelt among us, (and we beheld His glory, the glory as of the only begotten of the Father) full of grace and truth" (John 1:14, *KJV*). Some Christians living in a Hellenistic culture found it difficult to believe that God could be in the flesh like the rest of us.

I sometimes think that many Evangelical Christians tend toward becoming modern counterparts of the ancient Gnostics. While our theologically liberal opponents doubt the deity of Jesus, we have a tendency to diminish His humanity. We find it disconcerting and uncomfortable to view Jesus as fully human. We want to perpetuate the belief that He was different from the rest of us, that He had powers and knowledge that were super-human. We conveniently forget that He *learned* the Scriptures, *grew* into spiritual maturity and performed no mighty works in His own power (see Luke 2:52).

But God entered human history by giving up power in order to bring men and women into His kingdom through His love. He chose to redeem humanity and transform society through sacrificial self-giving, rather than through awesome demonstrations of power.

Jesus really did abandon power when He lived among us. He wasn't simply holding back and pretending to possess our physical limitations— He truly was one of us. Sometimes we react negatively to that fact and try to suppress it. We want to think of Jesus as a God who disguised Himself as an ordinary man but, at will, could step into a phone booth, rip off His robes and show us who He really was: a first-century Superman.

Judas refused to accept a limited Messiah. On Palm Sunday, power was within his Master's grasp. It was the logical time for a political take-over, so far as Judas was concerned. It was the opportunity to rally the masses to the cause; it was an hour when Jesus should claim power, and Jesus let it all slip away. Some think that Judas betrayed Jesus in order to force Him to play the power game when the Roman soldiers came to ar-rest Him—to force Him to establish His rule. This theory suggests that Judas felt that if Jesus were left with no alternative, He would overcome His reluctance to use power and seize the throne of Israel.

If that was Judas's plan, it backfired. Perhaps Judas hung himself when he realized that his attempt to manipulate Jesus ended in the death of the only One who had ever loved him unconditionally.

Jesus was not into power; there were no magic tricks up His sleeves. When mighty works were done through Him, He humbly admitted that He was not the one who deserved the credit. The glory belonged to the Father. In His miracles, we see God's love at work in the world—touch-ing those who were open to Him, never forcing or coercing. Again we see God limiting His power so as never to interfere with people's freedom.

WHEN RELIGION IS REALLY MAGIC

In time of trouble, we all want a God who will appear like a genie and magically make things right. We often want a superhuman masculine version of Mary Poppins to come floating into our lives just when we need Him, to take care of all the obnoxious details and difficulties. We ask ourselves: *What good can come from a God who empties Himself of power? What can such a God offer us? How does God think Jesus can get us to follow Him, if He doesn't destroy our enemies and establish the only kind of kingdom that people can understand?*

Recently, I was the speaker at a program marking the end of a train-ing program for inmates from some of the largest prisons in America.

They had come to know Christ while they were in prison and had been released for a three-week period to prepare themselves to witness to their fellow inmates, serving as evangelists within the prison system. This particular gathering marked the end of their preparation time, and there was an understandable sadness because these men knew that the next day they would be back in jail cells.

I had sat with them for several hours, listening to their stories. The agonies that marked their lives were almost too difficult for them to share. One man had raped and murdered a 10-year-old girl. His family had disowned him and his children hated him. He had not received a card or letter from any family member for years.

Another man told me that his mother was dying of cancer and that he was unable to be with her during her last days.

Still another shared with me that his wife had given up on him and had taken up with another man. His children had been taught to call her new spouse "father."

It was hard for me to hold back the tears as I listened to them.

Just before my opportunity to speak to the group, a guest soloist was introduced. She told the inmates that before she sang, she wanted to share a testimony with the group: "On the way here, I was driving my brand-new Ford. Unfortunately, I was right behind a dump truck filled with stones, and one of the stones fell off the truck, hit the road, bounced up onto my car and nicked my windshield. That made me *very* depressed. When I got out of the car, I looked at the nick on that windshield and I said, 'Lord, You know how unhappy this nick is making me.' Then I put my finger on the nick and prayed that Jesus would heal it. And would you believe, *He did*?"

The prisoner sitting next to me, along with several of his fellow prisoners, mumbled, "No!"

No wonder so many people don't believe in God. If God is ready to deal with the trivial while failing to alleviate monumental suffering, it's difficult to take God seriously. It is unbelievable that a loving God would turn a deaf ear to the passionate pleas of a repentant pervert and the agonized cries of a grieving son in prison, but then zip right down and heal a nicked windshield!

After the meeting, the soloist told me that the men didn't get their prayers answered because they didn't end them with the correct verbal formula: "In Jesus' name." She actually believed that the God of glory could be manipulated into performing magic tricks on our behalf if we employ the right incantation.

To imagine God as a magician-like deity who will give us what we want if we just use the right words makes God small. That's certainly what that woman soloist did. Preachers of a prosperity theology who regularly declare that God can make people healthy and rich if only certain formulas and practices are followed are guilty, in my estimation, of much the same.

In contrast, people recognized as saints of the Church are those who submit themselves to whatever God wants to do through them. When Jesus prayed to the Father, and said, "not my will, but Thy will be done," He obviously did not have magic on His mind.

WHAT DOES GOD OFFER?

I know what some people think: *If God can't be depended on to get rid of the dents in my fenders, to pay my bills or to help me find the best parking spaces, then what can I expect Him to do?* Or in a far more serious vein, *If God won't guarantee to cure my mother's cancer, bring about my child's salvation or keep a friend from being killed in Afghanistan, what good is He?*

The answer is *love*. God offers love—the empathy of love; the concern of love; the fellowship of love; the sharing of love. When you hurt, you can expect Jesus to hurt with you. When your heart is broken and the pain is unbearable, you can know that God's heart is broken in fellowship with yours. When, in agony, you cry, "My God, my God, why have You forsaken me?" God answers, "I know your agony. I share your sense of aloneness. I am with you."

God weeps with those who weep and suffers with those who suffer. Lovers always do, and God is the Lover of our souls. Love suffers long and is kind. Love patiently endures all things, bears all things, and believes all things (see 1 Cor. 13:5-7). Perfect love drives out all fears (see 1 John 4:18) and covers a multitude of sins (see 1 Pet. 4:8). Love never fails, even when everything else does. And when everything else has passed away, love remains (see 1 Cor. 13:8).

God is love, and love is what God offers you.

While on a speaking tour in England, I was asked to address a group of people in a community noted for its intellectuals. The person who had set up the meeting told me that some prominent peace-movement leaders, as well as a few Marxist intellectuals, would be present. My address was supposed to make Christianity credible to those with sophisticated commitments to the social sciences.

At the conclusion of the meeting, I invited anyone who wanted to talk further about Jesus to remain because I would make myself available for discussion. One very bright woman stayed and talked with me, and I expected her to try to show the flaws in my presentation, critiquing my remarks from a Marxist perspective. She had the style and vocabulary of many of the intellectuals I've met on campuses around the world. We talked briefly and then I asked her, "Why can't you believe in God?"

She stopped talking, and I noticed that tears were gathering in her eyes. She said, "I have never been married, but I have been pregnant. I wanted to have that baby more than anything else I have ever wanted. But when my baby was born, he had spinal meningitis and soon was dead. I couldn't believe that a loving God would allow such a thing to happen. If God loved me and loved my baby, and if God had the power to save my baby's life, why didn't He?"

I touched her shoulder and said, "God offers you His love, not His power. God did not save your child, not because He didn't want to, but because He chooses to be in our world in the weakness of His love rather than in the strength of His power. Yet I know that if you cry, God cries with you. When your heart is broken, God's heart is broken, too. Whatever agony you experience, with God it is far more. As much as you loved your baby, Jesus loved him more. I do not offer you a theological explanation for why this terrible thing happened. Instead, I offer you a Jesus who shares your sorrows and your pain. I offer you a Jesus who wants to bear your burden if only you will let Him. I very much want you to accept a Jesus who comes not in power, but with a broken heart."

She did! She was enticed not by the power of God, but by the God who comes as a suffering friend in Jesus Christ.

When Jesus taught us how to pray, He told us to address God as "Father" (see Matt. 6:9). The Hebrew word for "father" is *Abba*. It is a word that carries with it a sense of intense intimacy and is roughly akin to our word "daddy." The apostle Paul used the same word in his Epistle to the Romans when describing our relationship to God: "For you did not receive a spirit that makes you a slave again to fear, but you received the Spirit of sonship. And by him we cry, 'Abba, Father!'" (Rom. 8:15).

To the ancient Jews, the suggestion that YHWH could be addressed as "Daddy" must have seemed like blasphemy. Indeed, the idea has the same effect on many contemporary church people who are trained to talk to God as a majestic transcendental potentate.

I personally appreciate the formalized petitioning of the Almighty that marks many Christian worship services, and I was trained to use the proper formal ascriptions to God in prayer. However, I cannot imagine my son walking into my home when he was a teenager and saying to me:

O thou chairman of the Sociology Department at Eastern College,
O thou who doth clothe me, feed me and provide me
with every good and perfect gift,
I beseech thee this day—lend me the car!

He has never talked to me that way for a very simple reason: I am his dad and we are intimate. He hugs me, he kisses me and he talks to me as a son talks to his dad.

God wants a relationship with you that is even closer than that.

God wants to be closer to us than anyone else could ever be. He wants us to remain—to abide, to dwell—in Him, and He in each of us (see John 15). Many people who believe in Jesus and have an orthodox set of beliefs have never come to know God that way; they have not grasped the wonder and ecstasy of being personally loved by God. They are impressed by God's creative power when they look upon the majesty of creation, but they do not know that in Christ God laid aside the garments of His station and humbly invites them into loving intimacy.

There are some who prefer an awesome potentate whose countenance is too glorious to behold, and whose holy Ark of the Covenant demolishes any who would touch it. For me, it is good news that the Great One who is "past finding out" has humbled Himself and come to us, not in power, but in love (see Job 36).

I love the God who is ever waiting to be confronted on an old rugged cross. Weak and frail, suffering and battered, the God of time and eternity even now invites each of us to love Him as the crucified One; the One who has demonstrated His love for us by laying down His life. The God revealed in Jesus is very much a friend in an infinitely intense way. The God of creation manifested in Jesus has made Himself vulnerable, open to hurt and rejection; and in so doing has become a God who is very personal. We are invited, as was the apostle Paul, to enter into such intimacy with Him that we experience His sufferings and thereby are made into persons willing to give up power as we learn to love (see Phil. 3:10).

I want to be perfectly clear about this. Please do not misunderstand me. I am not saying that God lacks the power to perform miracles or that the testimonies of godly people who tell how God miraculously intervened in their lives during times of trouble are delusional. God is God and can do what He wants wherever and whenever He wants. But the Bible tells us that God has freely chosen to set aside that power to win us to Himself. Our God does not seek to overawe us with wonders and miracles, but rather seeks to draw us to Him by revealing Himself as a sacrificial lover. In Christ, God says, "But I, when I am lifted up from the earth, will draw all men to myself" (John 12:32). Thus, we are drawn to a God who presents Himself to us not as the One who can put the stars in space and set the earth spinning on its axis by His power, but as a broken Man spiked spread-eagled to a Roman cross outside a city wall.

At the cross, I am drawn to love Him. As I close my eyes and envision Him riveted there with nails through His wrists and feet, with the spear wound in His side, I want to cry for Him and with Him. When I visualize the crown of thorns tearing His skin and the blood and sweat running mingled over His contorted face, I want to reach up and wipe His brow. As I listen to the cries from His parched throat, I want to press a cup of cool water to His lips. He seems so tired and frail that I wish I could have carried His cross for Him. And then I hear Him say, "You can! You *can* carry My cross. And unless you do, you cannot be part of My kingdom." Seeing Him there, I find myself ready to do just that.

AN AFTERTHOUGHT ABOUT MIRACLES

Having made the case as best as I can for a God who prefers to be loving rather than omnipotent, I nevertheless want to affirm that I still believe in miracles. But I believe that miracles happen because of love rather than through the use of power. I began to believe this under the influence of Don Argue, one of the most respected Evangelical leaders in America and a prominent spokesperson for the Assembly of God denomination. He explained to me that a long-standing interpretation of what happened to Christ on Calvary's cross 2,000 years ago can affect healings in people's lives in the here and now.

Most Christians believe that when Jesus was crucified, He absorbed into His own personhood our sins; He cleansed us from all condemnation (see 1 John 1:9), yet many Pentecostals claim He did even more than that. They believe that when He hung on the cross, He was able to reach across time and space and absorb sicknesses. They base this belief on Isaiah 53:3-4, which reads:

He was despised and rejected by men, a man of sorrows, and familiar with suffering. Like one from whom men hide their faces he was despised, and we esteemed him not. Surely he took up our infirmities and carried our sorrows, yet we considered him stricken by God, smitten by him, and afflicted.

I am enough of a mystic to believe that such things are possible.

WHEN GOD DOES HIS STUFF

I have emphasized the love of God so much that it may sound as if I am suggesting that God does not use power at all. This certainly is not the case. While God chooses to set aside power to establish loving relationships with us, God still has awesome power at His disposal—and that power is, at times, put to great use.

Hopefully, I have made it clear that the loving God incarnated in Jesus is reaching out to us in love. I want to go on to affirm, in no uncertain terms, that this Jesus is coming back again, and when He does return, He is coming back in power. In Matthew 24, Jesus makes it clear that His *second* coming will be marked by hard judgment on those who have refused to be transformed by His love. Jonathan Edwards, the early American Puritan preacher, in his classic sermon "Sinners in the Hands of an Angry God," described that Day of Judgment wherein those who reject the love of Jesus will have to endure, through the exercise of His power, terrible condemnation.

The God who, by speaking, can create a universe out of nothing and can make the armies of the earth come to naught is also a God who can annihilate the world at a stroke. My claim is not that God does not have power, but rather that in order to express love, God in Christ set aside power, became a sacrificial lamb on a cross and is among us in these present days as One who comes in love.

Power is used by God, not so much for redemptive purposes, but to bring judgments to bear. God redeems, renews and heals through love, but uses power to destroy what refuses redemption and to consume whatever and whomever, in rebellion to His will, become enemies to His goodness.

To use words that some modern sophisticates might deem medieval (but which are nevertheless biblical and true), God will use His power to destroy the works of the devil (see 1 John 3:8). He will use His power to destroy the demonic forces that are now at work in the world and to extinguish the diseases and other evils that are evident in our fallen universe. With powerful fire, God will one day consume all that is worthless in this world; that which the Scriptures compare to "wood, hay or straw"—that is, things that cannot withstand God's holy presence. With that same fire, God will purify what is good and those who long to be in His presence; they are compared to "gold, silver and precious stones" (see 1 Cor. 3:11-15).

POWER OVER SIN

God may be self-limited from accomplishing all the miracles we ask of Him, but God is never limited in the power to enable us to overcome sin and temptation. The Holy Spirit's power must be exercised in our personal lives if we are to be purged of destructive tendencies and traits that prevent us from being the new creations we in fact are already in Jesus Christ. Each of us must overcome the lusts of the flesh and the "will to power," both of which are all-too-evident in our lives. All of us, sooner or later, find ourselves unable to control, by the sheer determination of the will, what we think or do. But we are taught in Scripture that in our weakness, through the power of the Holy Spirit, we will be able to be more than conquerors over anything that tries to keep us from becoming the persons we are meant to be (see Rom. 8:37).

The apostle Paul explains to us in Romans 7:19-24 that the things he knows he ought not to do and ought not to think, too readily become a part of his life; whereas the good that should be expressed in his thinking and in his actions often fail to be realized. He then goes on to make it clear that, through the power of the Holy Spirit, victory over his dark side can be achieved so that it no longer controls his thoughts and actions, thus freeing him to live out the good and perfect will of God.

You don't have to be a Freudian psychologist to be cognizant of the incredible hold that illicit sexual desires can have over any one of us. Lust seems to be evident at the core of human existence apart from Christ. In my own case, I find that my own willpower is not sufficient to combat such things. But then I find help from God to overcome such dark tendencies. I cry out, "God! Your property is in trouble! Deliver me!"

If there is any promise of God that is guaranteed, it is that those who call on the Lord in such times *will* experience deliverance. The Holy Spirit empowers Christians to win spiritual victories that otherwise would have been impossible. Let me again affirm that though God chooses not to be omnipotent, He is still a God who empowers.

One day, I was talking with a group of men at a Christian businessmen's luncheon. The struggles I have had with lust came up in our discussion. I shared with them honestly, telling them how I am tempted intensely and regularly to yield to sexual gratifications that would destroy me. After the meeting, one of the men came up to me and said he was shocked that they allowed me to be a speaker at a Christian gathering. He went on to explain that because he was "saved," these kinds of temptations never happened to him—and because they happened to me, he wasn't sure that I was really a Christian.

I resisted the urge to call him a liar and tried to explain that temptation is not sin, but rather *yielding* to temptation—deciding to do what the lusts of the flesh entice us to do—is sin. But he would not buy my explanation. He could not accept the reality that struggles against temptation are ever-present.

Fortunately, Jesus understands what I'm talking about. What is more, as shocking as this may seem to some, He had to endure the same temptations. There are those who, from the beginning of Church history, have tried to suggest that Jesus was not faced with such inclinations. But the Bible is clear when it states that He was tempted *in all ways that we are tempted*—and yet was without sin (see Heb. 4:15). Personally, I believe that Satan worked on Jesus more than on any other person in history; the evil one knew that if he could get Jesus to yield to temptation, he would conquer all of creation in one single coup. (Thankfully, that didn't happen!)

Undoubtedly, Jesus' constant praying was the source of the spiritual empowerment to overcome the temptations that buffeted Him at every turn. In prayer, He called on His Father rather than trusting in His own strength. He leaned on the One who had sent Him into the world in weakness. Through the power of God through prayer, Jesus won victories over temptations. But He didn't stop there; He declared that this same power would be given to any who asked for it (see John 1:12).

God is sufficient to meet all our needs for living victorious lives. Through the power of the Holy Spirit, we can be "more than conquerors" (Rom. 8:37). Those who seek to overcome temptations and addictions to sin through willpower alone soon find that without the Holy Spirit, they are doomed to failure.

I alluded earlier to the apostle Paul's struggle with temptation. He wrote in Romans 7:19-24:

> For what I do is not the good I want to do; no, the evil I do not want to do—this I keep on doing. Now if I do what I do not want to do, it is no longer I who do it, but it is sin living in me that does

it. So I find this law at work: When I want to do good, evil is right there with me. For in my inner being I delight in God's law; but I see another law at work in the members of my body, waging war against the law of my mind and making me a prisoner of the law of sin at work within my members. What a wretched man I am! Who will rescue me from this body of death?

To this question, Paul found the answer: God's power. He wrote:

Thanks be to God—through Jesus Christ our Lord! So then, I myself in my mind am a slave to God's law, but in the sinful nature a slave to the law of sin (Rom. 7:25).

EMPOWERMENT TO OVERCOME ADDICTION

There are a host of addictions that plague us, but in order to show how God can empower people to overcome "the power of cancelled sin and set the prisoner free," let us look at an addiction that is all too common among Christians. I am referring to the addiction to food.

Mark Twain once said, "Giving up smoking is the easiest thing in the world. I know because I've done it thousands of times." The same could be said about overeating. People who are appalled by what confronts them when they look in the mirror often resolve to take off weight by bringing their eating habits under control. Sadly, almost all of them fail.

Over the last few decades, there has been a growing awareness that overeating is not only a hygienic problem, but can be a spiritual problem as well. It is not by accident that *gluttony* was listed by the medieval church as one of the seven deadly sins. The sin of overeating is even more offensive in the context of a world inhabited by five hundred million malnourished and hungry people. We make light of the sin of overeating as though it were simply a bad habit and not an abomination in the eyes of God. It's hard for us to grasp the fact that in any 24-hour period, somewhere around 35,000 children die of either starvation or from diseases related to malnutrition.

Everywhere I go in America, I meet people who are obese. While there may be medical problems that cause people to be overweight, in most cases people are overweight because they eat too much, and what makes this especially deplorable is that they do so in a world wherein an unhealthy proportion of the population eats too little. Many people have told me that they have tried to diet, but just don't have the willpower to fight the desire to overeat. To them I can say, "The good news is that God can empower you to overcome your inclination to overeat."

When we read the Old Testament prophets, we find much condemnation in their messages when addressing those who have become overweight through overeating. Consider the words of the prophet Amos, who wrote:

Hear this word, you cows of Bashan on Mount Samaria, you women who oppress the poor and crush the needy and say to your husbands, "Bring us some drinks!" The Sovereign LORD has sworn by his holiness: "The time will surely come when you will be taken away with hooks, the last of you with fishhooks. You will each go straight out through breaks in the wall, and you will be cast out toward Harmon," declares the LORD (Amos 4:1-3).

There is no question that the prophet Amos had strong feelings about the overweight women of Bashan. I am amazed at how many ministers take to the pulpit with their fat stomachs hanging over their belts, not realizing that they are displaying a lack of control when it comes to their eating habits. They do not recognize that their obesity sends out a message of sin, even as they call their hearers to repentance for other sins.

I know it will upset many obese people to realize that their eating habits can be an affront to God. Well, they should be upset! The Bible says that their bodies are to be treated as sacred and to be regarded as temples of God (see 1 Cor. 3:16-17; 6:19). To hurt the "temple of God" through overeating is sin. Hence, overeaters should be upset. They should be so upset that they repent and ask God to provide them with the power to overcome the sin of gluttony.

Oral Roberts, the television evangelist and university president, was severely criticized when he instituted a program at his school to end obesity among his students. He required that all who matriculated at his school who were overweight would have to go on a diet and enter into a special program of exercising until they had their weight under control. Many of those who criticized Roberts thought his policy was for cosmetic purposes—that he did not want unattractive people on his campus. But such critics missed the point. Oral Roberts was justifiably concerned about the tendency toward obesity that he saw as all too evident among the Christians on his university's campus.[1]

In the eighth chapter of Romans, we read that knowing the law of God (that is, knowing what is right) is not enough, because human nature is such that people prove themselves too weak to do God's will when it comes to such things as sexual addictions or food addictions (see Rom. 8:1-9). But that same chapter indicates that Christ enables those who surrender themselves to an indwelling presence of the Holy Spirit, and that they will find that power comes from beyond themselves to overcome what otherwise would have been impossible.

Any person can access the Spirit of God through prayer, but there are some spiritual exercises that may prove especially useful. In a previous chapter, I wrote about St. Ignatius's "centering prayer," and I believe this method is especially effective for those who need a direct experience of the Spirit's powerful presence. If I keep at it day after day, I find that I am empowered to overcome and "throw off everything that hinders and the sin that so easily entangles" (Heb. 12:1). That power is the Spirit's presence. The infilling of God's Spirit gives me both the will and the power to do His good pleasure. The Holy Spirit's presence not only generates a powerful desire to overcome habits I had only weakly striven to overcome, but also provides the inner fortitude necessary to resist the temptations that so easily beset me. God's power can destroy what must be destroyed, even as God's love can redeem and renew what must be redeemed and renewed.

In overcoming addiction, it is especially helpful to enter a 12-step program such as Alcoholics or Overeaters Anonymous. One of the 12 steps is to believe that a "higher power" can be depended on to restore sanity and balance where none exists. The 12-step process also places great emphasis on support groups. Getting individuals to "carry each other's burdens" is a biblical calling (Gal. 6:2), and some churches have started 12-step programs as part of their ministries to address addictions of various kinds. As group members hold each other accountable and make themselves available for support in times of temptation, individuals experience God's deliverance: They are empowered to overcome the sin that would have overcome them had they continued to struggle alone.

THE POWER TO FORGET THE PAST

One evening several years ago, I preached in a small church in Indiana. Following the service, a young couple approached and asked if they could talk with me. They were about to end their marriage, and the wife thought that through counseling they might find a way to save it. I sat down with them in a small room adjacent to the sanctuary, and as I listened to their story, it was clear that their trouble lay in the young man's failure to be sexually faithful. He had entered into an adulterous relationship, and though it had ended, there were many wounds in the heart of his wife that had not healed. As we talked, he openly confessed what he had done and, with tears running down his cheeks, he begged for forgiveness. I sensed that the Holy Spirit was at work in his life, convicting him and convincing him that he had to change. What is more, I sensed that he was committed to allowing the power of God to enable him to overcome his lustful temptations. Over and over, he begged his wife for another chance, even as he cried out to God for forgiveness.

As best I could, I assured him that God would forgive him because, as it says in Romans 8:38-39, there is nothing that can separate us from the love of God. I told him that our God is a God who, "if we confess our sins, is faithful and just to forgive us our sins and cleanse us from all unrighteousness" (1 John 1:9). He surrendered his life to Christ. When our counseling session ended and the young couple left to go home, I was absolutely convinced that they were well on their way to the kind of reconciliation that would restore their marriage and make it even better than it was before.

Two years later, I was back in the same community for another speaking engagement. After I had finished my sermon, the young couple again approached and asked if they could spend a little more time visiting with me. I was thrilled at the opportunity and assumed that the husband's new life in Christ had ushered in a satisfying relationship between the two. I thought they had come to thank me for the counseling that I had given them a couple of years earlier, and I was preparing myself to accept all the compliments and praise I just thought were coming my way. However, when I asked how things were going, the young man said, "It's been hell!"

I was surprised and said, "I thought you became a Christian the last time we were together, and I thought that would have changed you and led to the resolving of your marital difficulties."

"I did become a Christian," he said. "My life *has* been changed and I've tried to be a good husband. Since the last time I saw you, I have been completely faithful to my wife."

"It's me," the young wife interjected. "It's me! I can't forget what he's done. I can't forget those other women. Every time he touches me, I think of where those hands have been and what they have done, and I cringe. I can't help remembering that other women have been in his arms."

I said, "You must forget. You must not only forgive, you must also forget."

"I can't," she said.

"I know," I responded. "But I believe that God has the power to destroy the harmful memories of the past. I believe that the Holy Spirit can purge your mind of the hurt and pain of the past. I believe that God can root out of your consciousness what keeps you from loving your husband. Why not ask the Lord to use His power to destroy the memory of those ugly things that torture you?"

I wish the story had a happy ending, but it doesn't. She never did allow the Spirit of God to work the miracle of forgetfulness in her heart and mind. She maintained what the Bible calls "the root of bitterness," and it ate away at her soul (see Heb. 12:15). The couple eventually divorced, but I believe that divorce could have been avoided. God could have destroyed the ugly images and memories that were in her mind, if she had given God the chance.

Don't we all need the purging power of God? Don't we all need to have the memory of certain things wiped from our consciousness? Don't we all realize that the memory of past hurts inflicted on us must be removed, just as cancerous tumors must be removed from a sick body if health is to be restored?

The good news is that God can obliterate the ugliness of our yesterdays, freeing us up to love in the present and in the days that lie ahead.

There is no doubt that when God forgives us, He forgets (see Jer. 31:34), and Jesus makes it clear that if we are not willing to accept God's power to do the same, we should not expect forgiveness on the Day of Judgment (see Matt. 6:14-15). When we pray the Lord's Prayer, we ask God to forgive us our sins even as we have forgiven the sins of others. As wonderful as God's forgiveness and deliverance are, we must access the Holy Spirit's power if we are to experience the joy and spiritual wholeness God intends for us. This means forgiving others and forgiving ourselves.

I once heard an evangelist shout at his audience, "On Judgment Day, God will play a videotape and project up on a screen images of all the sins you have ever committed. Every filthy, dirty thing you have ever done will be up there in full view—and your mother will be there!"

By the time he finished, I was more afraid of going to heaven and having to view that videotape with my friends and my mother than I was of going to hell. The good news is that there is no such video. If there were, I needn't be afraid because Jesus erased the tape. My sins are blotted out; they are buried in the deepest sea—*they are remembered no more!* (See Heb. 10:17.) That's the way God forgives, and God calls on us to forgive others even as He has forgiven us. Without the empowering presence of the Holy Spirit, it's impossible to do that; but with God's power, it is possible. God, who forgets what should be forgotten, empowers us to do the same.

LIVING WITHOUT POWER

I have been trying to make the case that the Christian alternative to power is *love*. Sadly, wherever I go, I meet people suffering from a lack of love. Such persons live out their lives in quiet desperation, devoid of the quickening vitality that only love provides. Sometimes they are bitter, but in many cases they are just emotionally dead. They walk and talk; work and play; eat and sleep—but they are devoid of life and energy. Without love, people die emotionally. They die because they are unwilling to reveal their needs, unwilling to let anyone know how desperate they are to be loved. They are afraid that such revelations will result in a loss of face; that people will no longer respect them; that they will lose the image of themselves as self-sufficient and powerful.

I know of a lonely Christian social worker whose life is without love. She has spent over 20 years serving the needs of people in an inner-city settlement house. She has sacrificed wealth, a family of her own and the benefits of middle-class living in order to meet the needs of the poor who have come to her for help. She has been honored as a public servant, received plaques and citations from an array of community organizations, and has been acknowledged as one of the most influential leaders of her city. Nevertheless, this woman suffers from loneliness. She complains that people admire her, but do not love her.

The reason this social worker experiences an absence of love in her life was expressed by one of her co-workers: "She is willing to do anything for other people, but she won't let anybody do anything for her. She is unwilling to let others know she needs them."

Unless we show our need for others, we cannot be loved by them. Unless we allow people to give to us, we cannot have a love relationship with them. Unless we reveal that we are powerless to meet our own emotional needs and are open to the love of others, there is little hope that we will experience the love we have been created for.

This woman was afraid to reveal her needs because she was afraid of losing power. Powerful people convey the impression that they do not depend on anyone for anything. Consequently, people do not reach out to them in love. This woman defined herself as self-sufficient, as powerful people generally do, and cut herself off from those who would have loved her if they knew she needed their love.

Giving is a gift of the Spirit that is imparted to some Christians (see Rom. 12:7), and an unwillingness to receive what others want to give denies them their ability to exercise their spiritual gift. The Bible says that it is more blessed to give than it is to receive (see Acts 20:35), but allowing others to give to us allows *them* to enjoy the blessing of giving. If we present ourselves as people who need nothing from others, we deny them the blessings they would receive in giving their love to us.

Recently, a missionary told me that he was not returning to the mission field because he did not have the necessary financial support to sustain his work. He told me that he was quite willing to give everything he had to the people he served on the field, but he had a difficult time asking for support from church people here in the United States. He just could not bring himself to let people know of his needs. He was afraid of being beholden to anyone.

That missionary thought I would laud him for his attitude toward money. Instead, I had to tell him, as gently as I could, that he had been seduced by power. "By being the giver," I explained, "you exercise power over the receivers. Yet you are unwilling to be a receiver because you think it will make you appear powerless to meet your own needs. Receiving requires a humility that people who crave power do not have."

It is not only more blessed to give than to receive—it is easier, too. Receiving requires humility. It requires a revealing of need. It requires an acknowledgment that we are powerless to help ourselves. The powerful shy away from receiving; giving is their thing—but never receiving. Those of us who love power will give help to anyone who asks for it. Giving makes us feel in control and makes the people we have helped obligated to us. Giving feels so good that some of us will help almost anyone, often without asking enough questions.

There have been countless rip-offs by instigators of pseudo-charities, who exploit people's desire to give. A student conducted an experiment as part of a course he was taking in sociology. Wanting to test people's willingness to give, he stood on a street corner with an unmarked can in his hand. For a week, people who passed him put over $20 a day into that can. He discovered that it does not take much to get people to give—giving does not threaten the power status of the giver.

Receiving, however, is seldom a power play.

WHO IS YOUR NEIGHBOR?

One of the most familiar parables of Jesus is also one of the least understood: the story of the Good Samaritan. Jesus told this story in response to a lawyer who wanted to know how to gain eternal life. Jesus reminded him that eternal life belongs to those who love their neighbors as themselves. The lawyer responded by asking another question: "Who is my neighbor?" To answer him, Jesus told this story:

A man was going down from Jerusalem to Jericho, when he fell into the hands of robbers. They stripped him of his clothes, beat him and went away, leaving him half dead. A priest happened to be going down the same road, and when he saw the man, he passed by on the other side. So too, a Levite, when he came to the place and saw him, passed by on the other side. But a Samaritan, as he traveled, came where the man was; and when he saw him, he took pity on him. He went to him and bandaged his wounds, pouring on oil and wine. Then he put the man on his own donkey, took him to an inn and took care of him. The next day he took out two silver coins and gave them to the innkeeper. "Look after him," he said, "and when I return, I will reimburse you for any extra expense you may have." Which of these three do you think was a neighbor to the man who fell into the hands of robbers? (Luke 10:30-36).

Usually when preachers preach from this passage they make the point that our neighbor is anyone who is in need and, as Christians, we should respond by giving of ourselves to meet their needs. However, I am not sure that this is the only point Jesus was making. Jesus asked, "Which of these three do you think was a neighbor *to the man who fell into the hands of robbers?*" I think that the answer is, *the one whom the man let help him out of his desperate situation.* The parable, I believe, shows us that we express neighborly love to others by letting them bind up our wounds, lift us out of the gutter and care for us. In presenting himself as weak and vulnerable and willing to trust the Samaritan, the robbed and beaten man was loving. As I read it, in receiving help from the Good Samaritan, the man who had fallen among robbers expressed love for him.

Think of the times you have been in need and were desperate for help. Remember how lonely you felt? Wasn't it then that you realized how few friends you really had? Did you realize then that a true friend is someone you love enough to turn to when you need help?

You may be willing to give help to anyone, but when you yourself are in desperate need, it's likely that you only ask for help from people you love. You let that person know that you love him or her by asking for help, and you honor that person in your request. You say, in essence, "Out of all the people I know, you are the one I will trust with the revelation of my need. You are the only one to whom I dare expose my inadequacies. You are the one I love."

It could be said that that poor man didn't have much choice about who helped him. And yet I have seen people with far more freedom of choice than he had who have refused to take the help available from man or God. I believe this parable reflects light not only on our relationships with other people, but also on the nature of our relationship with God. We show love for God when we are willing to accept salvation as a gift. Our love for God is demonstrated not so much in what we do for God, but in our willingness to allow God to do for us what we cannot do for ourselves.

The apostle Peter learned this complex lesson when Jesus tried to wash his feet in the Upper Room.

[Jesus] got up from the meal, took off his outer clothing, and wrapped a towel around his waist. After that, he poured water into a basin and began to wash his disciples' feet, drying them with the towel that was wrapped around him. He came to Simon Peter, who said to him, "Lord, are you going to wash my feet?" Jesus replied, "You do not realize now what I am doing, but later you will understand." "No," said Peter, "you shall never wash my feet." Jesus answered, "Unless I wash you, you have no part with me." "Then, Lord," Simon Peter replied, "not just my feet but my hands and my head as well!" (John 13:4-9).

Peter wanted to do something for Jesus, but was reluctant to allow Jesus to do anything for him. He needed to be taught that he could show love by allowing Jesus to serve him.

Trying to earn our salvation through good works means that we want to do something for God so that God will be obligated to us. It puts *us* in a position of power. Grace, on the other hand, is when we love God enough to receive the precious gift offered to us in Jesus Christ. Without question, this puts us in a state of obligation and gratitude. We are called on to respond with good works in Christ's name to those in need, because of the gift provided for us at Calvary. We will always be indebted to God.

LIVING WITH LOVE

As I come to the end of this book, I want to share with you some simple actions that will allow you to experience the joy that comes from creating and giving love.

The first action is to *listen*. There are few things that can create love between persons like attentive listening. I am not referring to the kind of half-hearted listening that characterizes so many of our daily exchanges; I mean the kind of listening where you energetically give yourself to the person who is speaking—you hang on their every word, intensely relate to their feelings and empathize with everything they say. It is the kind of listening that not only *hears* what the persons says, but *listens* to what they mean. Often people mean far more than they say. Listening that leaves the listener exhausted from self-giving renews them through the creative power of love.

When I was a seminary student, I pastored a small church in New Jersey. As part of my pastoral responsibility, I visited the people of my congregation. Much to my surprise, I discovered that several of the women in the church were falling in love with me. Please don't get the idea that I have some exaggerated concept of my own personal attractiveness; I am well aware that I am a very average-looking man. My nose is long and my imminent baldness was already quite evident, even in those early years of ministry. These realities made me all the more surprised when several women seemed to feel romantically inclined to me.

Reflecting on their feeling many years later, it is clear to me what happened: The women were married to insensitive men who came home from work, sat in the living room, watched television, called it a day and went to bed. The wives hungered for meaningful conversation—most of all, they craved somebody who would listen. As a young pastor, I met that need. I gave earnest attention to their every word. After an hour of hanging on their every word and looking meaningfully into their eyes, it shouldn't have come as a surprise to hear, "You know, I don't think I have ever felt this way with a man before." I was doing what their husbands should have done: listening with the kind of listening that creates love. Is it any wonder that so many people fall in love with their counselors and psychotherapists?

Jesus' capacity to listen is in evidence throughout the Gospels. He was the greatest Teacher who had ever lived, the Man who had more of importance to say than any other in history. Yet above all else, He gave time to the ministry of listening. He heard the sick when they told Him of their troubles; He listened to the petty gripes and squabbles of His disciples; He heard the cries of the demon-possessed with a concern that no one had ever demonstrated before. Jesus listened, and sin-sick souls were renewed. To love as a Christian means listening as Jesus listened.

The second action that creates love is *showing concern for the happiness of the other person.* A husband should wake up in the morning and ask himself, "What can I do today to make my wife a happier person?" and then set himself to the task of doing those things. The more he does to make his wife happy, *the more in love with her he will be.* It's as simple as that. (The same process should be employed by a wife who wants to create love with her husband.)

Many of us think we must love people first and then, because we love them, do good things for them. In reality, the opposite is true. The more good we do for people, the more we love them. The Bible says, "For where your treasure is, there your heart will be also" (Matt. 6:21). This means that what a person invests in, he or she loves. If a person invests in a relationship, makes sacrifices for it and provides every consideration for the other person's needs, that person is creating love.

Yet we tend to believe that *after* we love somebody, we then invest in the relationship. In reality, we love somebody *because* we already have invested in the relationship. My wife and I often talk about the love we have for each other and how it came into existence. We have also concluded that the reason why we love each other is that over the years, each of us has given so very much to the other. Love did not just happen; it was created through sacrifices and self-giving on each of our parts. The more each of us invested ourselves in our marriage, the more precious the relationship became and the deeper the love between us grew.

A friend of mine tells a story about a man who was falling out of love with his wife. This husband was advised by a marriage counselor to think of all the ways he could make life happier for his wife and then to do them. A few days later, the counselor received a telephone call. The husband said, "Every day I leave for work, put in a hard day, come home dirty and sweaty, stumble in the back door, go to the refrigerator, get something to drink and then go to the rec room to watch television until supper time. After talking to you, I decided I would do better than that in the future. So yesterday, before I left work, I showered and shaved and put on a clean shirt. On the way home, I stopped at the florist and bought a bouquet of roses. Instead of going in the back door as I usually do, I went to the front door and rang the doorbell. My wife opened the door and I handed her the flowers and told her I love her.

"She took a long look at me, and started to cry. When I asked her what was wrong, she said, 'It's been a horrible day. First, little Billy broke his leg and I had to take him to the hospital to have his leg put in a cast. I no sooner returned from the hospital then your mother called and told me that she is coming to stay for three weeks. I tried to do the wash and the washing machine broke and there is water all over the basement floor . . . *and now you come home drunk!*' "

In some marriages, such thoughtful consideration is so unusual that it's easy to understand how a wife could think her husband was drunk because he was so good to her. But it shouldn't be that way! When we do loving things for someone, we become more loving. What we do changes our own hearts.

The third and most important action that creates love is *recognizing that Jesus is present in the other person*. Those who recognize Jesus' real presence in the people they meet find it easy to love others in spite of their shortcomings, weaknesses and frailties. When, by the grace of God, you can look past another's nasty behavior, cruelty and eccentricities and see Jesus mystically incarnated within them, love becomes possible.

FINDING JESUS IN THE OTHER

In J. D. Salinger's book *Franny and Zooey*, there is a brilliant passage that communicates the way I believe God can be encountered in another person.[1] In the story, Franny comes home from college psychologically messed up because of her involvement in a strange religious cult. Her beliefs are confused, her perception of reality is distorted and her ability to relate well to people is gone. Her brother Zooey tries to bring her back to health by reminding Franny of the time their family had a radio show; in preparation for the broadcast, their older brother, Seymour, would always tell them to shine their shoes, straighten their clothes and do their very best for "the fat lady."

Zooey asks Franny what had come to her mind when Seymour said that. In his own mind, Zooey explains, he saw a picture of a fat lady sitting on a porch, swatting flies, with her radio going full blast from morning until night. He saw her sitting there in the terrible heat of a summer day, suffering from cancer. Whenever he pictured her, he wanted to do his very best on the radio show, because he was doing it for that lady. He hoped that, if he were good enough, she would forget her pain and loneliness and lose herself in the excitement of the radio program.

In response, Franny explains that she had a similar image. While she didn't see the fat lady on a porch, Franny did imagine her as having thick, veiny legs and, like Zooey's fat lady, her's was suffering from cancer, too. Franny goes on to explain that she also wanted to do her very best to help the fat lady.

Zooey responds, "And don't you know who that fat lady really is? . . . Ah, buddy. Ah, buddy. It's Christ Himself. Christ Himself, buddy."

When I read that passage for the first time, written by an author who is by no means on the Evangelical speakers' circuit, I was startled that Salinger had grasped something so profound: God is a presence waiting to be encountered in every person. God is in the fat lady, in the skinny man, in the oppressed African-American, in the difficult neighbor, in the male chauvinist and in the downtrodden victim of the social system. God is in every one of them, and in every other person I meet; in my son, my daughter, my wife, my colleagues and my friends, Jesus waits to be encountered.

It is easy to love someone when you realize that he or she is not simply what meets the eye. In a real yet mystical way, each person is imprinted with the indelible image of God. No wonder the apostle Paul instructed us to see each other no longer in the flesh, but to view each other in the spirit (see 2 Cor. 5:10).

I do a bit of marriage counseling, and every once in a while I talk to a married person who no longer loves his or her mate. Often such a person says to me, "You either love somebody or you don't. You can't make yourself love somebody. You can't make love happen." Such a person is usually trying to escape the guilt associated with having sworn love and faithfulness "until death do us part" and trying to evade responsibility for their disintegrating relationship. *It's not my fault*, they insist—the death of love *just happened*.

I have never been too sympathetic to the denials of such people, for I am convinced that people *can* make themselves love. Jesus commanded us to love, and in so doing, He let us know that love is a matter of the will. He taught what our most advanced insights into human personality only confirm: that love can be created by people who make a commitment to listen to each other, to care for each other and to recognize in each other the presence of the eternal God.

I believe that love is greater than power. Only love redeems us and makes us good.

SOME CONCLUDING WORDS

You probably noticed that this is not one of those books that makes you nod your head in agreement with everything you read. I have not sought here for agreement as much as I have tried to express my own struggles with questions and problems as I try to make sense out of how love and power have played themselves out in my life. This I have done with the hope that some of what I have said will help you as you deal with these very same questions and struggles. There is no expectation on my part that you will agree with all that I have written because, as the Bible says, each of us must work out his or her salvation with fear and trembling (see Phil. 2:12).

The theme of this book is of significance because of the interplay of love and power that lies at the intersection of understanding the gospel. The God who sets aside power in order to live out love, fully expressing that love on Calvary's tree, is at the core of the Christian message to the world. The failure to probe the meaning of Jesus' refusal to yield to Satan's temptation to use power to establish His kingdom rule through economic, religious or political power is a mistake that leads us to distort the gospel. Not only will we not understand the way Jesus sought to bring His kingdom to earth as it is in heaven, but we are likely to distort the image He presented of His heavenly Father.

I also have tried to point out, if only to a limited extent, that how we deal with the most pressing issues of our times—war, environmental degradation, political conflicts, international relations—depends on how we choose to handle power.

I have tried to show how the more personal and "closer to home" matters—how we relate to each other in the home; whether or not marriages succeed; how our children are raised; whether or not we as individuals become the people that God wants us to be—are deeply entwined with the ways we deal with love and power. Struggling to allow love to trump power will determine if our homes will become havens in a heartless world, or become, as is too often the case, places marked by destructive conflict. Such struggling ought not to be avoided.

This is demonstrated through the parable about the schoolboy who was given an assignment to solve some math problems. He found that it was much easier to solve those problems if he first looked in the back of the textbook where the answers were listed. "Working out" the problems by first having the answers made it so much easier for him, but it was no way for him to develop into a proficient mathematician.

So it is with developing as a Christian. To accept the answers to life's problems as given by some theologian or counselor may make things easier, but it prevents development into mature spirituality. That's why I do not ask for passive acceptance of what I have written, but humbly ask that you think through for yourself the issues I have raised. I hope that you will do so with your Bible in one hand and this book in the other. If you find that there is no biblical basis for what I have written or if you think my use of the Bible may be erroneous, go for what you believe the Bible is telling you. The Bible is an infallible guide for faith and practice. What I have written is not.

This book has been difficult for me because so little has been written that explores the relationship between love and power. The work of philosophers, sociologists and theologians on this topic seemed very limited, and I found scarce resources from which I could critique my own thinking and writing. In some ways, I had the sense that I was plowing new turf, which left me feeling that I could easily encounter pitfalls—and I probably did. Nevertheless, the subject matter seemed so important that I was convinced I ought to take the risks.

It is my hope that this book will lead you to others' thoughts and writing on the relationship between love and power. I believe that increased understanding within the Church on this relationship will improve life, not only for ourselves, but also for the world God so desperately loves and calls us to love.

ENDNOTES

Preface to the New Edition
1. Phillip Rieff, *The Triumph of the Therapeutic: Uses of Faith After Freud* (New York: Harper & Row, 1966).

Chapter 1: Power Plays in the Peaceable Kingdom
1. Max Weber, *The Theory of Social and Economic Organization* (New York: Oxford University Press, 1947).
2. See "Dietrich Bonhoeffer" at Christianity.com. http://www.christianity.com/Christian%20 Foundations/The%20Essentials/11536759/ (accessed September 2009).

Chapter 2: Love and Power in the Family
1. Christopher Lasch, *Haven in a Heartless World* (New York: Basic Books, 1978).
2. Willard Walter Waller, *The Family: A Dynamic Interpretation* (Wilmington, MA: Holt, Rinehart and Winston, 1951).
3. Edgar Friedenberg, *Coming of Age in America* (New York: Random House, 1965).
4. Deborah Tannen, *You Just Don't Understand: Women and Men in Conversation* (New York: William Morrow & Company, 1990).

Chapter 3: Women with Power
1. Marabel Morgan, *The Total Woman* (Grand Rapids, MI: Fleming H. Revell Co., 1975).

Chapter 4: When Children Get Power
1. Dennis A. Ahlburg and Carol J. DeVila, "New Realities of the American Family," *Population Bulletin,* vol. 47, no. 2, August 1992; Meyer F. Nimkoff and William F. Ogburn, *Technology and the Changing Family* (Boston, MA: Houghton Mifflin, 1955).
2. U.S. Census Bureau Press Release, "Single-Parent Households Showed Little Variation Since 1994, Census Bureau Reports," March 27, 2007. http://www.census.gov/Press-Release/www/releases/ archives/families_households/009842.html (accessed September 2009).
3. Erik Erickson, *Childhood and Society* (New York: W.W. Norton and Company, 1963), and *Identity, Youth and Crisis* (New York: W.W. Norton and Company, 1998).
4. Émile Durkheim, *Suicide: A Study in Sociology*, translated by John A. Spaulding and George Simpson (New York: The Free Press, 1951).
5. Research paper by Kathleen Johns, University of Pennsylvania, January 1967, for A. Campolo, visiting professor.
6. Ibid.
7. Stephen R. Covey, "Strengthening Families in Times of Crisis," May 8, 2008. http://www.stephen covey.com/blog/?tag=family-mission-statement (accessed September 2009).

Chapter 5: Religious Power Plays
1. Bronislaw Malinowski, *Magic, Science and Religion and Other Essays,* Joseph Needham, ed. (New York: The MacMillan Company, 1925).

Chapter 6: Holy Terrors
1. William Golding, *Lord of the Flies* (New York: Berkley Publishing Group, 1962).
2. "Christianity in China: Sons of Heaven: Inside China's Fastest-Growing Non-Governmental Organization," *The Economist*, October 2, 2008. http://www.economist.com/world/asia/display story.cfm?story_id=12342509 (accessed September 2009). Some internal estimates put the number as high as 130 million.
3. Kwame Bediako, "Africa and Christianity on the Threshold of the Third Millennium," *African Affairs*, 99 (2000).
4. Ibid.

Chapter 7: Glorious Authority

1. See www.radio-locator.com.
2. Lisa Leff, Associated Press, "Donors Pumped $83M to Calif. Gay Marriage Campaign," via ABC News, February 2, 2009. http://abcnews.go.com/US/wireStory?id=6790538.
3. Martin Luther King, Jr., *Strength to Love* (New York: Harper & Row, 1963).
4. "And Can It Be that I Should Gain?" words by Charles Wesley (1738), music by Thomas Campbell (1825).
5. "Ten Thousand Angels," words and music by Ray Overholt (1958).
6. President Reagan's story was an adaptation of Charlotte M. Yonge, "The Last Fight in the Colisaeum," from *A Book of Golden Deeds* (London: Blackie & Son, Ltd., 1864).

Chapter 8: Rulers in the Upside-Down Kingdom

1. *The Works of Plato*, selected and edited by Irvin Edman (New York: The Modern Library, 1928), pp. 397-480.
2. Georges Sorel, *Reflections on Violence*, translated by T. E. Hulme (New York: The Free Fress, 1950).

Chapter 9: What to Do While We Wait for the Second Coming

1. Amy F. Woolf, "Nuclear Weapons in Russia: Safety, Security and Control Issues," *CRS Issue Brief for Congress*, April 12, 2002. See also Faithful Security: The National Religious Partnership on the Nuclear Weapons Danger, www.faithfulsecurity.org.
2. From an interview by Jim Wallis and Wes Michaelson, *Sojourners*, August 1979. http://www.sojo.net/index.cfm?action=magazine.article&issue=soj9611&article=961110 (accessed September 2009).
3. John Stott, from a sermon preached in All Souls' Church of England, Langham Place, London, 1979.
4. Ronald J. Sider and Richard K. Taylor, *Nuclear Holocaust and Christian Hope* (Downers Grove, IL: InterVarsity Press, 1983). Used by permission.
5. David Rieff, "Were Sanctions Right?" *New York Times*, July 27, 2003. http://www.nytimes.com/2003/07/27/magazine/were-sanctions-right.html.
6. Philip Yancey, "Gandhi and Christianity," *Christianity Today*, April 8, 1983, p. 16.

Chapter 10: The Sins of the Powerless

1. Martin Buber, *Ich und Du* (1923), first English translation, 1937.
2. Deborah Tannen, *He Said/She Said: Women, Men and Language* (Recorded Books, Barnes and Noble, 2003).
3. Otto Pollock, *Social Science and Psychotherapy for Children* (New York: Russell Sage Foundation, 1952).
4. John Perkins, graduation address at Eastern University, May 2000.
5. R. C. Sproul, *Surprised by Suffering* (Grand Rapids, MI: Tyndale House Publishers, 1994).

Chapter 11: The Painful Cost of Conquering Love

1. Harold S. Kushner, *When Bad Things Happen to Good People* (New York: Random House, 1981).
2. Abraham Heschel, *The Prophets* (New York: Harper and Row, 1962), pp. 285-298.
3. "Jesus Shall Reign," words by Isaac Watts (1719), music by John Hatton (1793).
4. These fanciful stories appear in The Infancy Gospel of Thomas.

Chapter 12: When God Does His Stuff

1. From a conversation with Thomas Dahlstrom, registrar at ORU in 1982, dated October 6, 2009, at St. Davids, Pennyslvania. Thomas reported that this program was in place and that if students did not comply, they were expelled.

Chapter 13: Living Without Power

1. J. D. Salinger, *Franny and Zooey* (New York: Little, Brown and Company, 1961).

ACKNOWLEDGMENTS

I am one of the few authors these days who does not use a computer. What I write, I write longhand. Then I send my scribbling to my associate and typist, Sarah Blaisdell. She in turn works through a host of edits made by my personal assistant, James Warren. Working with him is Robert Gauthier, his associate. All three of them deserve heaps of gratitude for what they have done to make this book possible.

Great gratitude goes to Aly Hawkins, editor at Regal Books, who carefully read, corrected and edited this book.

Finally, a special thank you goes to my wife, Peggy, who gave up hours and hours that belonged to her. She lovingly sacrificed, allowing me to invest what this book required.

ALSO FROM
TONY CAMPOLO

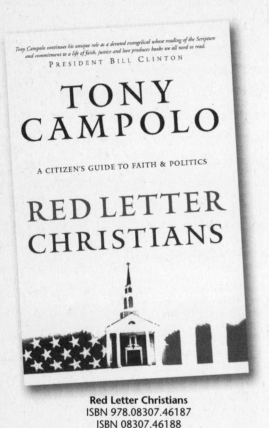

Red Letter Christians
ISBN 978.08307.46187
ISBN 08307.46188

Over the past couple of decades, evangelical Christians have often been associated with the Religious Right and the most conservative positions of the Republican Party. Rebelling against this designation are those who prefer to be called "Red Letter Christians," desiring to live out the red letters of Jesus' words in the New Testament. Believing that Jesus is neither a Republican nor a Democrat, Red Letter Christians transcend partisan politics and concentrate on issues viewed critically through a moral and biblical lens. In *Red Letter Christians*, Tony Campolo examines many of the hot-button issues facing evangelicals from the perspective of Jesus' red-letter words in the Bible. These include the environment, war, the AIDS crisis, Palestine, education, gun control, the role of government and choosing the right kind of candidate. No matter where you fall on the political spectrum, Campolo will make you think, pray and act.

With *"Campolian" passion and insight*, Red Letter Christians *prods, challenges, questions, invites and instructs us to be people who love and live the words of Jesus.*

BRIAN MCLAREN (brianmclaren.net)